EXECUTING *the* BASICS *of* Healing

A GAME PLAN FOR WALKING IN DIVINE HEALTH

D0064515

EXECUTING *the* BASICS *of* Healing

A GAME PLAN FOR WALKING IN DIVINE HEALTH

KENNETH W. HAGIN

Unless otherwise indicated, all Scripture quotations are taken from the *King James Version* of the Bible.

21 20 19 18 17 16 15   11 10 09 08 07 06 05

Executing the Basics of Healing:
A Game Plan for Walking In Divine Health
ISBN-13: 978-0-89276-739-7
ISBN-10: 0-89276-739-1

In the U.S. write:
Kenneth Hagin Ministries
P.O. Box 50126
Tulsa, OK 74150-0126
1-888-28-FAITH
rhema.org

In Canada write:
Kenneth Hagin Ministries of Canada
P.O. Box 335, Station D
Etobicoke (Toronto), Ontario
Canada M9A 4X3
1-866-70-RHEMA
rhemacanada.org

CONTENTS

1. Brushing Up on the Basics 1

2. God's Will Is Healing. 5

3. 'The Lord That Healeth Thee'. 27

4. Healing Belongs to You. 45

5. Two Methods of Receiving Healing 57

6. God's Word Is Medicine. 77

CHAPTER 1

———

BRUSHING UP ON THE BASICS

Often when ministers in the "word of faith" movement begin a sermon by saying, "I'm going to teach on the subject of healing," most people in the congregation will say to themselves, *I already know about healing.* Well, people may think they already know all there is to know about healing, but when there's a healing line, more than half the congregation will get in the line for prayer. That tells me they don't know as much about healing as they think. Or that they don't know how to walk in the light of what they know. Now don't misunderstand me. I'm not saying that ignorance about healing is what causes people to get in the prayer line. Rather, it is not knowing enough about healing and living in divine health that causes them to get in line repeatedly without receiving a lasting result.

No matter how well we know a subject, if we don't continue to practice or review what we know, we will forget some things. For example, after taking two years of typing class in high school, I became a fairly decent typist. Eventually, I joined the U.S. Army and was able to use the Teletype in Army communications. However, that was many years ago, and, in recent months, as I've started using e-mail on my computer, I've noticed that I am not as proficient a typist as I used to be. I did not keep my skills sharp through regular practice, so I lost some of the typing skills I once had.

A person may have acquired spelling, math, or computer skills, but if he hasn't used them in a while, when he does try to use them, he discovers that his skills are rusty. The same thing can happen in spiritual matters. You see, many Christians know about the subject of healing, but they're not as proficient in healing as they could be—simply because they haven't practiced what they know. In other words, they don't continually study the subject and act on what they have already learned.

There are certain subjects we need to brush up on continually, and healing is one of them. Unfortunately, when a minister begins to teach on the subject of faith or healing or another subject we've heard a lot of teaching on, some Christians think to themselves, *Oh, I already know about that.* And then they tune the preacher out, so to speak. In other words, they think they've already heard all there is to hear on the subject, so they quit listening to the message. But we need to remember that we may not be as proficient in our knowledge as we could be. Besides, it never hurts anyone to review what he has learned.

My dad, Rev. Kenneth E. Hagin, often tells the story about a certain man who heard him preach many years ago. This man was an elder in one of the churches where Brother Hagin held regular meetings. The man had heard Brother Hagin preach on Mark 11:24 many times. After one service in which Brother Hagin shared from Mark 11:24, this man said to him, "That's the thirteenth time I've heard you preach on Mark 11:24, and I finally got it."

You see, sometimes it takes us a while to "get it." In other words, sometimes we need to hear something more than once before we really get hold of it and fully understand it.

In this book I want to cover the basics and lay a foundation on the subject of healing. Some teaching may be review for many readers and brand-new for others.

Through this teaching, you can begin to formulate a game plan, so to speak, for walking in divine health. A "game plan" is simply *a strategy for achieving an objective*. Our objective is to walk in divine health, and our strategy for achieving this goal must be based on God's Word.

As we learn what God's Word says on the subject of healing, we can learn how to execute the basics of healing in our own lives and begin walking in divine health.

CHAPTER 2

———

GOD'S WILL IS HEALING

In discussing the basics of healing, the first issue I want to address is the way the Church generally understands sickness and healing. And when I say "Church," I am referring to the Body of Christ as a whole, not to any specific denomination. The primary line of thinking concerning sickness is, "I am sick for a reason; this is just God's will." Or "God has put this sickness on me to teach me a lesson."

In the New Testament, did Jesus ever put sickness on anyone? When people came to Him for healing, did He ever say, "No, it's not My will. Just suffer a little longer"? No! Not one time!

JOHN 14:8-14 (*NIV*)
8 Philip said, "Lord, show us the Father and that will be enough for us."
9 Jesus answered: "Don't you know me, Philip, even after I have been among you such a long time? ANYONE WHO HAS SEEN ME HAS SEEN THE FATHER. How can you say, 'Show us the Father'?
10 Don't you believe that I am in the Father, and that the Father is in me? The words I say to you are not just my own. Rather, it is the Father, living in me, who is doing his work.
11 Believe me when I say that I am in the Father and the Father is in me; or at least believe on the evidence of the miracles themselves.

12 I tell you the truth, anyone who has faith in me
will do what I have been doing. He will do even
greater things than these, because I am going to
the Father.

13 And I will do whatever you ask in my name, so
that the Son may bring glory to the Father.

14 You may ask me for anything in my name, and I
will do it."

The emphasis of this passage of Scripture is about
knowing God. Philip wanted to know God the Father.
He even asked Jesus to show the Father to him and the
other disciples. Jesus answered his request by saying,
"Anyone who has seen Me has seen the Father" (v. 9).
In other words, Jesus was saying, "If you want to know
what God is like, look at Me."

If we want to see God at work, all we need to do is
look at Jesus. If we want to know what the will of God
is, we can look at Jesus and the works He did in His
earthly ministry.

It doesn't make sense for people to say that God puts
sickness on people when Jesus has said, "If you've seen
Me, you've seen the Father." You see, if God the Father
puts sickness on people, then Jesus would have had to
put sickness on people when He was on the earth. And,
if God puts sickness on people, Jesus would have had
to refuse to heal some during His earthly ministry, saying, "No, God put that on you for a reason." If God puts
sickness on people, then Jesus was lying when He said,
"If you've seen Me, you've seen the Father." But in the
New Testament we find Jesus only healing people.

WHO *IS* TO BLAME FOR SICKNESS?

Well, since God doesn't put sickness on people, who does? There are people in this world today who are sick and dying, so it's important for us as Christians to know exactly where sickness comes from—so we can help people better understand and receive healing.

> **ACTS 10:38**
> **38 How God anointed Jesus of Nazareth with the Holy Ghost and with power: who went about doing good, and healing all that were oppressed OF THE DEVIL; for God was with him.**

This passage of Scripture says that Jesus went around doing good and healing the sick. But notice that this verse not only identifies the One doing the healing, but it also identifies the one making people sick. Does it say that Jesus was healing all who were oppressed of *God*? No! It says Jesus healed all who were oppressed of the *devil*. Now you know why blaming God for sickness and disease doesn't make sense!

Sometimes people make up reasons why people are sick simply because they can't figure out why their Aunt Jane or Uncle Joe or some other friend or relative didn't get healed. Sometimes, the individual was a godly Christian who believed in divine healing, but for some reason didn't receive healing. So everyone close to him tries to figure out why he didn't receive healing. When they can't figure it out, they make something up. They come up with the idea that God must have made the person sick for a reason.

That kind of reasoning is similar to the way people talk about salvation at testimony meetings. Some people will stand up and testify, "God had to take everything away from me so He could get me saved." No, He didn't! After they lost everything because of the devil, they probably stopped, reflected, and then turned to God. But they could have turned to God while they still had everything!

Sometimes when one member of a family is sick, people think the reason is so everyone in the family will turn to God. That is wrong thinking. God doesn't make people sick for any reason.

It is difficult for man to understand some things just using his natural thinking. For example, it is often difficult for people to understand why such bad things are happening in the world today. But we need to look at things from a biblical viewpoint. When the laws that God has established are violated, bad things often happen. But that doesn't mean it's God's will that those things happen.

Many people talk as if God is the author of the bad things that happen in the earth. But is God really causing accidents, sickness, death, and so forth? Insurance policies even use the phrase "acts of God" to include storms, earthquakes, catastrophes, and other calamities. The people who attribute these things to God simply do not understand God's nature or His plan.

THE CURSE OF THE *LAW* AND THE CURSE OF THE *FALL*

As Christians, we have to realize that there is a difference between the *curse of the Law* and the *curse of the Fall*! You see, we have not been physically redeemed from the curse of the *Fall*, but we *have* been spiritually redeemed from the curse of the *Law* (Gal. 3:13). This is

where most Christians get confused in their thinking—
they do not understand this truth.

For example, women having to endure pain in
childbirth (Gen. 3:16) and men having to work "by the
sweat of his brow" (Gen. 3:19) are curses of the Fall.
Sickness and disease are curses of the Law—part of the
penalty for breaking God's Law or commandments (*see*
Deuteronomy 28). As I said, we are redeemed from the
curse of the Law. We are *not* redeemed from the curse
of the Fall.

Now I want to take a closer look at the story of the
Fall in Genesis chapter 3. To summarize the beginning
verses: God went into the garden looking for Adam and
Eve, but they had hidden themselves from Him because
they had sinned. God asked, "Why have you hidden?"

Adam answered, "We are naked," and God replied,
"How did you know that? You must have eaten from the
tree from which I told you not to eat."

Let's begin reading in verse 13.

GENESIS 3:13,14 (*NIV*)
**13 Then the Lord God said to the woman, "What is
this you have done?" The woman said, "The serpent
deceived me, and I ate."**
**14 So the Lord God said to the serpent, "Because
you have done this, "Cursed are you above all the
livestock and all the wild animals! You will crawl
on your belly and you will eat dust all the days of
your life."**

According to this passage, we know that in original
creation, the serpent was considered livestock. Also, this
passage indicates that the serpent originally walked
on four legs. Genesis 3:14 says, "You will crawl on your

belly," so, evidently, the serpent didn't crawl beforehand. In other words, if the serpent was already crawling on his belly, why would God then tell him after Adam and Eve sinned, "You're now going to crawl on your belly"? Likewise, why would He say, "you will be cursed above all livestock" if the serpent wasn't considered livestock? These verses indicate that God changed the serpent's nature and physical characteristics at this time.

Not only were the serpent's nature and physical characteristics changed at the time of the Fall, but the serpent was also *cursed*. The serpent became cursed because he allowed himself to be used by Satan.

> **GENESIS 3:15 (*NIV*)**
> **15 "And I will put enmity between you and the woman, and between your offspring and hers; he will crush your head, and you will strike his heel."**

And not only was the serpent cursed, but the man, the woman, and their offspring—all of mankind—were cursed at the time of the Fall.

> **GENESIS 3:16-19 (*NIV*)**
> **16 To the woman he said, "I will greatly increase your pains in childbearing; with pain you will give birth to children. Your desire will be for your husband, and he will rule over you."**
> **17 To Adam he said, "Because you listened to your wife and ate from the tree about which I commanded you, 'You must not eat of it,' "Cursed is the ground because of you; through painful toil you will eat of it all the days of your life.**
> **18 It will produce thorns and thistles for you, and you will eat the plants of the field.**
> **19 By the sweat of your brow you will eat your food until you return to the ground, since from it**

you were taken; for dust you are and to dust you will return."

The woman received a curse, the man received a curse, and the ground also received a curse. Even the earth was cursed! Romans 8:22 says, *"For we know that the WHOLE CREATION groaneth and travaileth in pain together until now."*

It's important to realize that the curses were caused indirectly by the devil. Therefore, when disasters and tragedies occur, no one should say, "God is the author of it all," because God is not the author! Satan is!

Remember, Jesus said in John 14:9, "He that has seen Me has seen the Father." Well, no one ever saw Jesus doing bad things. When we read the Bible, we don't ever see Him causing storms. No, He *rebuked* storms!

MARK 4:35-39
35 And the same day, when the even was come, he [Jesus] saith unto them, Let us pass over unto the other side.
36 And when they had sent away the multitude, they took him even as he was in the ship. And there were also with him other little ships.
37 And there arose a great storm of wind, and the waves beat into the ship, so that it was now full.
38 And he was in the hinder part of the ship, asleep on a pillow: and they awake him, and say unto him, Master, carest thou not that we perish?
39 And he arose, and rebuked the wind, and said unto the sea, Peace, be still. And the wind ceased, and there was a great calm.

In the middle of this violent storm, Jesus rebuked the wind, and it became still. Jesus wasn't rebuking something God had done! If He were, Jesus could not have honestly said, "If you have seen Me, you have seen God," because He and God would have been working against each other, and we know that's not true.

WHO IS THE GOD OF THIS WORLD?

We need to understand some things about the world's system. Adam was originally in control of this world in which we live. God had given him dominion to rule over it. In reading the Book of Genesis, we find that after God created Adam, He told him, "You're in control" (Gen. 1:26). In other words, God made Adam "god"—with a lower case "g"—over this world.

Now I want to make this point clear so that people won't misquote me, thinking that I am calling Adam God. When people say a person is acting like a god, they mean that he is acting as if he controls everything. When we study the Word of God, we discover that at the time of creation, Adam literally did control everything— because God had given him dominion!

God gave Adam control over all of creation! In other words, Adam was the caretaker underneath God Himself. You see, God made the world and the fullness thereof (Ps. 24:1), but then He put Adam in charge of it. In fact, when you study the Word of God, you discover that God didn't even name the animals. Adam named them (Gen. 2:19). (If you've ever wondered why a certain animal is called a certain name, it's because that's what Adam named it.)

Now let's look at Second Corinthians 4:4, because this verse states that *Satan* is the god of this world.

2 CORINTHIANS 4:4
4 In whom the god of this world hath blinded the minds of them which believe not, lest the light of

the glorious gospel of Christ, who is the image of God, should shine unto them.

In the last part of this verse, "God" is mentioned with an uppercase "G," which means it is referring to the divine Entity, Jehovah God Himself. Remember, whenever the word "god" with a lowercase "g" is used in the Bible, it is not referring to divinity or deity. It is only referring to deity when it is capitalized.

Second Corinthians 4:4 says that Satan is the god of this world. The Book of Genesis says that God gave *Adam* charge over this world, but here in Second Corinthians, Paul says that *Satan* has charge over it. When and where did dominion switch from Adam to Satan? At the Fall of man, when Adam gave in to Satan. In disobeying God, Adam also gave his dominion over this world to Satan. That's why the world is under Satan's control today.

I often hear people saying, "God has everything under control." Well, whether I agree or disagree with that statement depends on what they mean by it. If they mean to say that God is ruling the earth right now, then I would have to disagree with their statement, because He is not ruling the earth right now. He is going to rule one day in the future, but He's not ruling right now. But if by saying, "God has everything under control" they mean that He has everything *in their life* under control because they've submitted their life to Him, then I can agree with their statement.

But to say that God controls everything that happens in the world today is wrong and not a true statement. Because God's Word tells us to pray for people in authority—that they would make right decisions so that we would be able to live in peace (1 Tim. 2:1,2). God wouldn't tell us to pray for those in authority if He had control over all the people in government. God does not have control over everything or everyone in this world.

Often, when Christians differ in their ideas, it's only a matter of understanding the terminology they are using. You see, some Christian groups have religious jargon. So to avoid misunderstanding, it's important to clarify what we mean when we make certain statements. "God is in control of everything," is one such statement.

Yes, God has everything *in my life* under His control (and everything in *your* life, too, if you are committed to Him). But it's obvious that everything has not been placed under His control. God will only have control over this entire world after Jesus returns, puts down all rebellion, and establishes reign upon the earth (1 Cor. 15:24,25). At that time, everything and everyone will be at peace. No one will bicker with another, and the lamb will lay down with the wolf (Isa. 11:6; 65:25). That is the way it was when Adam first had control over the earth.

We must also remember that when God created the earth, He established certain *natural* laws, such as the law of gravity. From the moment God established these laws, the earth has been under their control, because that is the way God designed it. However, there are times when God, through the working of miracles, will suspend these laws for the benefit of mankind or for the good of His children.

GOD IS A GOOD GOD!

I'm reminded of an article that was written by a well-known newspaper columnist many years ago during the Korean War. The columnist said, in effect, "I don't claim to be a Christian, but I'm not an atheist or an agnostic, either. The atheist says there is no God. The agnostic says there may be a God; he doesn't know for certain. I believe there is a God. I don't believe everything 'just happened' into being. But what hinders me from becoming a Christian is hearing preachers say that God is running everything. Well, if He is, He's sure got things in a mess."

Then the columnist talked about wars, murder, abuse, poverty, sickness, disease, and so forth. He said, "I believe there is a Supreme Being somewhere, and that everything He made was beautiful and good. I can't believe these other things are the works of God."

Without realizing it, that man went right along with what the Word of God says. Remember, in Genesis 1:31 after God created the earth, He looked at all He had made and said it was good! And in James 1:17, God's Word says, "Every good and perfect gift comes down from the Father above."

You see, when we really study the Word of God and discover who God is and what God does, we learn there is no possible way He could be the cause of all the evil that people accuse Him of. That kind of thinking is contrary to what the Word of God says about His nature.

Then who causes all of this world's evil? Who causes sickness and disease? And who causes wars? *The devil does!* John 10:10 says that the devil has come to steal, kill, and destroy. That verse isn't just referring to the spiritual realm. The devil has come to steal, kill, and destroy in this natural world!

Understanding that Adam committed high treason in the Garden, sold mankind out to the devil, and that this world is under Satan's control, it is very obvious why evil things are happening in the world today.

When we take into account Jesus' description of the Father and Jesus' own actions while He was here on the earth, there is no possible way that God could be involved in causing sickness and disease, wars and killings, and accidents and catastrophes! So, who *is* in charge of all that evil? The devil is.

If Christians would just get their thinking straightened out, it would help straighten out their theology. But the problem is, their theology is already messed up; therefore it messes up their thinking until Satan is able to wreak havoc in their lives. As my father has taught for years, right *thinking* produces right *believing*, which produces right *results*. On the other hand, wrong thinking produces wrong believing, which produces nothing but negative results.

GOD'S HEALING NATURE

The devil and his foul offspring—sin, sickness, doubt, and unbelief—are trying to rob Christians of God's many blessings. One way a Christian is robbed of God's blessing of healing is by blaming God for the sickness! But, as I said, when you know what the Bible has to say about the nature of God and the nature of the devil, there is no doubt who the author of sickness is.

Let's briefly look in the Bible at the progression of teaching on the subject of healing. God established a covenant of healing with His people in the Book of Exodus. The Israelites had come out of the bondage of Egypt to a place called Marah, and they couldn't drink the water there because it was bitter. The people began to murmur against Moses. Exodus chapter 15 records the story.

EXODUS 15:23-26
23 And when they came to Marah, they could not drink of the waters of Marah, for they were bitter: therefore the name of it was called Marah.
24 And the people murmured against Moses, saying, What shall we drink?
25 And he [Moses] cried unto the Lord; and the Lord shewed him a tree, which when he had cast into the waters, the waters were made sweet: there he made for them a statute and an ordinance, and there he proved them,
26 And said, If thou wilt diligently hearken to the voice of the Lord thy God, and wilt do that which is right in his sight, and wilt give ear to his commandments, and keep all his statutes, I will put none of these diseases upon thee, which I have brought upon the Egyptians: for I AM THE LORD THAT HEALETH THEE.

From this chapter, we find through our study of healing that the very nature of God described in the Bible refutes the idea that God makes anyone sick.

Let's read Acts 10:38 again. It says, *"How GOD anointed Jesus of Nazareth with the Holy Ghost and with power. . . ."* Also, John 14:10, which says, *". . . the Father that dwelleth in me, HE doeth the works."*

Jesus healed when He was on the earth, not because He was the Son of God, but because He was *anointed*! He didn't minister healing because He was deity; He healed in His humanity—as a human anointed by God!

Now we know that Jesus was anointed by God, but what exactly did Jesus do once He was anointed with the Holy Ghost and with power? Notice that Acts 10:38 does *not* say, "Jesus went about doing good and making sick those who God said were supposed to be sick and healing those who God said were supposed to be well." It also does not say, ". . . healing *half* of the sick and leaving the rest of them."

No, Acts 10:38 says Jesus received that anointing from God and went about doing good and *healing*! Healing who? All who were oppressed *of the devil*. You see, this ties in with the fact that God had given Adam dominion and rule, which Adam turned over to Satan. That's why Satan is called the god of this world (2 Cor. 4:4). And it's the god of this world who is oppressing and destroying.

God is the Deliverer. God is in the healing, helping, and restoring business, not in the sickness, hurting, and destroying business.

God's Word says, ". . . *all who were oppressed of the devil . . .*" (Acts 10:38). The truth can't be stated any more plainly than that! And yet many people who are sick still say, "Well, you know, God's trying to teach me something."

God's Word says that Jesus healed all who were oppressed of the devil, which means everyone who was healed under the ministry of Jesus was oppressed of the devil. So God doesn't use sickness to teach people lessons. The devil uses sickness to steal, kill, and destroy people! The devil who was oppressing people in the Bible is the same devil who is oppressing people today. The good news is, the power and the anointing of God that healed those oppressed by the devil is the same power and anointing healing people today!

Don't misunderstand me. Just because someone is oppressed by the devil does not necessarily mean there is an evil spirit present in that person's body. There might be, and there might not be. There could be an evil spirit present enforcing sickness, but there does not have to be.

This fact needs to be very plainly understood. (Of course, the devil is always the author of sickness.)

NO EXCEPTIONS!

If, for a moment, we go along with what some people believe, and we say God is the author of sickness and disease, then God and the devil must have changed places at some point in history between the time that the Bible was written and now. I am basing that statement on what the Bible clearly says about God, the devil, and sickness and disease.

MARK 16:18
18 They [believers] **shall take up serpents; and if they drink any deadly thing, it shall not hurt them; they shall lay hands ON THE SICK, and they shall RECOVER.**

If some people are sick by God's design so He can teach them a lesson, how can we know which ones to lay hands on and which ones to leave to God's "design"? It would be impossible to know who to lay our hands on and who not to lay our hands on.

If it is true that some individuals are supposed to be sick because God wants to teach them something, then Mark 16:18 should read, "Lay hands only on the ones I authorize you to lay hands on, because I want only those to recover. But tell all the other sick people that they are supposed to remain sick."

Jesus didn't say that! He said, "Lay hands on *the sick*," period! There are no other qualifications and no exceptions to the rule!

When I was in school, many times when the teacher was explaining a grammar or spelling rule, she would say, "Always do such-and-such, *except* under certain circumstances." For example, to help the students remember how to spell certain words, the teacher would say, "Use 'i' before 'e' except after 'c'"!

It seems there is an exception to every rule in the natural. But notice that Mark 16:18 simply says, "Lay hands on the sick"—with no exceptions!

SHOULD CHRISTIANS SUFFER?

Someone might say, "But Second Timothy 2:12 says we should suffer."

2 TIMOTHY 2:12
12 If we suffer, we shall also reign with him: if we deny him, he also will deny us.

This passage of Scripture says that we are to suffer with Jesus and that if we suffer with Him, we can reign with Him. First, we need to determine exactly what the word "suffer" is referring to. Did Jesus suffer sickness? Did He suffer pneumonia, cancer, or some other kind of disease? No! What did Jesus suffer? *Persecution.*

Many of us were persecuted—either by friends, family, or others—when we chose to live for Jesus. Persecution for the Word's sake or for following Jesus is the kind of suffering that this passage of Scripture is talking about!

Sometimes people will concoct silly theologies in an attempt to explain circumstances they can't understand. But, friend, I'm going to tell you right now, there is no preacher alive who has the explanation for every situation. Personally, I have prayed for many people who didn't receive their healing. But I have prayed for many more people who did receive their healing! And no matter who doesn't receive, I'm not going to quit praying. You see, I have preached to many people who needed salvation, but they didn't get saved. I'm certainly not going to quit preaching salvation because some people don't receive. I'm also not going to try to make up a reason why people choose not to receive Jesus!

I'm always going to preach the truth about salvation *and* healing. The Word of God is so simple, yet sometimes we try to make it theologically profound. I've even heard people say, "It can't be that simple." Yes, it can! Jesus said it was.

'IS ANY SICK AMONG YOU?'

Now that we have dealt with questions about Second Timothy 2:12, let's look at another passage of Scripture that proves healing is the will of God.

> **JAMES 5:14**
> **14 Is any sick among you?** [Among who? Among those in the Church.] **let him call for the elders of the church; and let them pray over him, anointing him with oil in the name of the Lord:**
> **15 And the prayer of faith shall save the sick, and the Lord shall raise him up; and if he have committed sins, they shall be forgiven him.**

Notice verse 14 asks, "Are there any sick among you?" To me, this question implies that there should not have been any sick among them. In other words, being sick was not the expected, normal occurrence. Otherwise,

James wouldn't have to ask if there were any sick; he would have just known or assumed that there were.

This passage goes on to tell us what to do if there are any sick, which means we aren't to just leave them sick, thinking God is trying to teach them something. This verse says to call for the elders of the church, anoint the sick with oil, and pray the prayer of faith; then the Lord will raise them healed and whole!

Let's look again at some misunderstood verses when it comes to the issue of God's will concerning healing.

HEBREWS 12:6
6 For whom the Lord loveth he chasteneth. . . .

Notice this verse does not say, "Whom the Lord loves He *makes sick*." Some people try to make this verse say that! Actually, the Greek word translated "chasten" means *to child train* or *educate*. In modern language, we might use the word "discipline" instead of chasten.

Even natural parents discipline their children because they love them. But no parent disciplines his or her children by making them sick. To chasten is simply to "child-train" or to discipline.

I love my children, so I disciplined them when they were growing up. But I never made them sick! God never makes His children sick, either! He disciplines us and He trains us. He leads us and He guides us. But He never uses sickness to train us or teach us things.

WHAT ABOUT JOB?

Someone might say, "But, look at poor old Job. God made *him* sick." No, God didn't make him sick. The

Bible plainly says that the devil made Job sick. In Job chapter 1, the devil went to God and asked for permission to make Job sick. God answered him, "You have permission to do anything you want to do to him, except kill him."

It's important to understand that God didn't *commission* this to happen; He simply gave *permission* for it to happen. You see, what happened to Job was something that Job himself had greatly feared.

JOB 3:25
25 For the thing which I greatly feared is come upon me. . . .

It was Job's fear that brought the situation upon him. Fear is sin, and sin opens the door to the devil.

Remember, this account in the Book of Job did not take place over a long period of time. Bible scholars agree that everything that is recorded in the Book of Job took place in nine to eighteen months. So, if we take the worst-case scenario, the whole Book of Job took place in less than two years. And in the end, God turned Job's captivity!

JOB 42:10
10 And the Lord turned the captivity of Job. . . .

When someone is sick, he is captive to the devil. And if the devil steals everything from him, that person is captive to the devil. Job had lost everything he had, and he was terribly ill. Job was in captivity to the devil! But God turned Job's captivity and gave him *twice* what he had before!

We can rest assured that the enemy is going to try to attack us, because the Word of God records the fact that the enemy attacked God's people. But, we also read that if they were willing to stay with God and trust Him, they walked out victorious on the other side.

It's important to remember that healing is from God, and sickness is from the enemy, Satan. Anything evil that comes against us is from the enemy. We need to understand that the devil is the god of this world. And there is a difference between the curse of the Law and the curse of the Fall! Deliverance from the curse of the Law comes when a person is born again, but deliverance from the curse of the Fall does not come until Jesus returns.

Some Christians try to make you think that if you serve God and live by faith, you're going to live in a utopia—a place where you are never attacked by the devil, never sick, never in financial difficulty, and so forth. That just isn't so! As long as you are in this natural world where the devil is ruling, you will have tests and trials.

As Christians, we are living in a "utopia" only in the spiritual sense. But naturally and physically, we are still living under the curse of the Fall that God placed on this world when Adam and Eve sinned. We still have thorns and weeds to deal with in our yard! We still have to work in order to eat.

These things are all a part of the curse of the Fall. In the beginning, Adam didn't do anything except dress and keep the Garden (Gen. 2:15). But when he fell, when he sold out to the devil, he began having to toil and labor for everything that originally had just been given to him.

FREE FROM THE CURSE OF THE LAW

Even though we are still living under the curse of the Fall, we can stand against this world's problems and limit their effect in our life, because our spirit man is born again. But this world's problems are still going to exist and possibly affect us, because the curse of the Fall is still in effect until Jesus returns.

It's time that we teach along this line, because this subject has not been properly taught, and many Christians are trying to get redeemed from something they can't be redeemed from because it is a part of the curse of the Fall. No one will be released from the curse of the Fall as long as they are living on this earth. Romans 8:22 says the whole creation groaneth for that time when it will be released!

We have been released spiritually. Galatians 3:13 says we have been set free from the curse of the Law. But the curse of the fall is going to remain on this earth until Jesus comes. However, because we have been redeemed from the curse of the Law, we can lessen the effect of the curse of the Fall. But we need to remember that certain effects of the curse are going to be present as long as we're in this world.

Remember, God's nature is a healing nature. In other words, God's will is healing. We need to remember that Satan is the author of sickness and disease. God is the author of divine healing and health!

CHAPTER 3

———

'THE LORD THAT HEALETH THEE'

In the last chapter, we covered some very basic biblical truths about divine healing. We learned that God is not the author of sickness. Satan is the one who makes people sick, because he only comes to steal, kill, and destroy (John 10:10). We also read in Acts 10:38 that God anointed Jesus to heal people who were oppressed by the devil.

Healing has been God's idea from the very beginning. He has always been opposed to sickness. In the Old Testament, God made provision for healing for His covenant people (Exod. 15:26). I don't think God would have made provision for healing if He wanted people to be sick!

If God doesn't want His people to be healed, why did He make provision for it? It would be a waste of His time to spend a lot of time making provision for something that isn't His will. For example, in the natural, it's ridiculous to think that a boss would have an employee spend a lot of time making provision for something the company didn't want done!

It's easy to recognize that God's will is healing! Sometimes we just need to use some basic logic and think things through ourselves instead of letting everyone else tell us how it's supposed to be!

EXODUS 15:26
26 And [God] **said, If thou wilt diligently hearken to the voice of the Lord thy God, and wilt do that which is right in his sight, and wilt give ear to his commandments, and keep all his statutes, I WILL PUT none of these diseases upon thee, which I have brought upon the Egyptians: for I am the Lord that healeth thee.**

Some Hebrew scholars have said that the word "put" in this verse should actually be translated *permit*. And if you will study the Word of God in its entirety and in context, you will see that the word "permit" better agrees with the whole counsel of God's Word. So when we read this verse, "I will 'permit' none of these diseases. . . ," it reads more in line with the nature of God as we study the rest of the Bible.

Some people want to come against the so-called faith message because we teach so strongly on healing and faith, but I don't get into arguments with anyone about these issues. Likewise, I'm not going to argue with anyone over whether this verse should read "put" or "permit." But I do suggest something to those who would be skeptical. Before they throw the idea of "I will *permit* none of these diseases . . ." out the window, I recommend they study the entire Word of God and, as they do, examine the nature of God in context with other scriptures to see if it isn't more reasonable to use the word "permit" in this particular passage.

According to God's own Word, He doesn't make people sick! Remember, Acts 10:38, which says, *"How God anointed Jesus of Nazareth with the Holy Ghost and with power: who went about doing good, and HEALING ALL THAT WERE OPPRESSED OF THE DEVIL. . . ."* If God were making people sick, this verse would have to say, ". . . healing those who were sick because God had made them sick." No, the Bible is clear about the fact that Satan is the author of sickness and disease.

The Bible also says that a house divided against itself will not stand (Matt. 12:25). If God were the one making people sick, but then He turned around and anointed His Son to heal them, that would be an example of a house divided against itself.

You see, if we just use a little bit of common sense and keep the Word of God in context, we'll be convinced that God is not making people sick!

Also, notice that Exodus 15:26 says, "I am the Lord who heals you." He isn't the Lord who makes you sick! He didn't make the Israelites sick; He is the Lord who healed them! In this verse of Scripture, God reveals Himself to Israel as Jehovah Rapha, "the Lord who healeth thee."

We learned in chapter 1 that Satan is the god of this world. Remember, Second Corinthians 4:4 says, *"The god of this age has blinded the minds of unbelievers, so that they cannot see the light of the gospel of the glory of Christ, who is the image of God (NIV)."* The god of this age, or world, is Satan.

The devil is the one who makes people sick! Jesus is the One who heals. Healing has been God's idea from the very beginning.

COVENANT PROVISION

As long as Israel walked in the covenant they had made with God, He took sickness away from among them.

EXODUS 23:25,26
25 And ye shall serve the Lord your God, and he
shall bless thy bread, and thy water; and I will take
sickness away from the midst of thee.
26 There shall nothing cast their young, nor be
barren, in thy land: the number of thy days I will
fulfil.

One thing we need to remember when it comes to
serving the Lord is Deuteronomy 6:5, which says, *"And
thou shalt love the Lord thy God with all thine heart, and
with all thy soul, and with all thy might."* You see, this
is part of walking in covenant with Him.

Walking under the covenant is what keeps us from
being sick—or, in other words, keeps us living in divine
health. (You see, healing is needed only if we get sick!)

What do I mean by walking in the covenant? I mean
living wholeheartedly for God. I mean accepting Jesus
Christ as your personal Savior, being water-baptized,
and being filled with the Spirit and speaking with other
tongues according to Acts 2:4. I mean obeying God's
Word. That is living under the covenant!

THE BLOOD COVENANT

To help better understand our covenant, I want to
explain what a covenant is and give some examples of
natural covenants—covenants made man-to-man, not
God-to-man. *Webster's* dictionary defines "covenant" as a
*formal, solemn, and binding agreement; a written agree-
ment or promise usually under seal between two or more
parties, especially for the performance of some action;
pledge;* and *contract.*

Sometimes when children make pacts with their friends, they may even call themselves "blood brothers." When I was a teenager, I made a pact with three of my closest buddies.

The four of us have been friends since we were about eighteen years old. Even after all these years, we still get together sometimes to fellowship, and we stay in regular contact through e-mail.

Many people have made a pact, an agreement, or a covenant with a friend or group of friends. And these covenants are important. We value and honor them.

Well, God made a covenant with us! It's called the blood covenant! It was established when Jesus died on the Cross and rose from the grave. The covenant was ratified by the shed blood of Jesus Christ. In Matthew 26:28, Jesus says, *"For this is my blood of the new testament, which is shed for many for the remission of sins."* The blood Jesus shed wiped away our sins, and the New Covenant He established is still good today!

When you were born again, you entered into a covenant with God through the shed blood of the Lord Jesus Christ. And through His blood, provision was made for your healing.

OUR COVENANT OF HEALING

Many Christians only talk about Jesus' blood being shed for salvation. Yes, it was shed for salvation, but Jesus also bled when He received those thirty-nine stripes upon His back, because First Peter 2:24 says, "By His stripes we were healed." We know that through the blood Jesus shed when those stripes were laid upon His back, God provided healing for our bodies!

Isaiah 52:14 says that Jesus' countenance or appearance was so marred from the beating He received that He wasn't recognizable. Many commentaries and scholars give a very vivid description of the appearance of a man beaten as Jesus was beaten. They agree that the mutilation caused when the whip hit the back and wrapped around the body was devastating, ripping the stomach and the face.

It's easy to understand why Isaiah said that Jesus was hard to recognize. Jesus' visage was marred because of the beating He took. And because of His blood that was shed in that beating, we have a covenant of healing!

IF WE *WERE* HEALED, WE *ARE* HEALED!

In Chapter 1, we learned about the healing covenant God established with His people in the Book of Exodus. Remember, the Israelites had come to Marah, where they couldn't drink the bitter water, so they murmured against Moses. At the Lord's direction, Moses dipped a tree into the waters, and the waters immediately became sweet.

EXODUS 15:25,26
25 And he [Moses] cried unto the Lord; and the Lord shewed him a tree, which when he had cast into the waters, the waters were made sweet: there he made for them a statute and an ordinance, and there he proved them,
26 And said, If thou wilt diligently hearken to the voice of the Lord thy God, and wilt do that which is right in his sight, and wilt give ear to his commandments, and keep all his statutes, I will put none of these diseases upon thee, which I have brought upon the Egyptians: for I AM THE LORD THAT HEALETH THEE.

This passage holds great significance for Christians that we sometimes overlook. I want to show you how this covenant in the Book of Exodus foreshadowed the covenant Jesus fulfilled on the Cross.

Remember what is happening in this passage—God is making a healing covenant with Israel. At this time, the children of Israel had already passed through the Red Sea. Now they had come up to waters that were bitter. At the Lord's direction, Moses took a tree, and dipped it in the waters to "heal" the waters, and they became sweet.

We must understand types and shadows for this to mean anything to us. You see, the tree was a type of the Cross of the Lord Jesus Christ, and, at different times in the Bible, water was used to represent people. In the Old Testament, the covenant of healing was established when Moses took the tree and dipped it into the bitter waters. In the same way, the Cross of the Lord Jesus Christ—the broken body of the Lord Jesus Christ—dipped into the bitter waters of humanity established a covenant, which declared, "By His stripes you were healed."

1 PETER 2:24
24 Who his own self bare our sins in his own body on the tree, that we, being dead to sins, should live unto righteousness: by whose stripes ye were healed.

First Peter 2:24 says, "By Jesus' stripes, you were healed." It's not, "You're *going to be* healed." And it's not, "You *might be* healed." No, it says, "You *were* healed!" And if you *were* healed, then you *are* healed!

Some people say, "You're not supposed to change what the Bible says. First Peter 2:24, says *'were* healed.'" Yes, the verse says, "By His stripes you *were* healed," but we could read it as "*are* healed," and the meaning doesn't change at all. We can also say, "By His stripes I *am* healed," and the meaning still isn't changed! If we *were* healed, then we *are* healed!

Then there are some people who ask, "What does what happened in the Book of Exodus have to do with us? That was then and this is now." I always reply, "Well, what does *God* have to do with us today?" His actions have to be the same today as they were then, or He is not the same God. Malachi 3:6 says, *"For I am the Lord, I change not. . . ."* Therefore, if God was Jehovah Rapha to His children in Exodus, then He is still Jehovah Rapha to His children today. If He isn't Jehovah Rapha today, then He isn't the same God He was to Israel, which means He lied in Malachi 3:6 where He said, "I change not."

STIR UP WHAT YOU KNOW!

We need to get hold of some of these basic truths again. Too often, we let them go and forget what we've learned. Yes, we need to continue to grow and hear teaching on different subjects, but we also need to go back occasionally and recover what should always be familiar ground. This kind of review sharpens and strengthens us. For example, each time healing is taught, our faith for healing ought to grow stronger than it was before!

By way of illustration, everyone knows that if chocolate milk sits for a while, all the chocolate syrup will settle on the bottom of the glass. Therefore, it has to be stirred up before you can drink it. When the milk and the syrup get separated, you have to "shake it up"!

In the same way, we receive so much teaching on certain subjects, but, after awhile, some of the truths we knew so well at first begin to "settle down." Then the devil is able to take advantage of us, because the truth isn't stirred up within us. We have to continually go back and remind ourselves of what we have learned. This simply stirs up what is in us, making it more and more effective.

We need to stir up our remembrance about the healing covenant. And we need to realize that God is the same today as He was in the Old Testament! He was against sin in the Old Testament, and He is against sin today! He was against sickness in the Old Testament, and He is against sickness today. He made provision for healing in the Old Testament, and He has made provision for healing for us today!

THE BLESSINGS OF GOD

There are certain blessings God has said belong to those who serve and obey Him. These blessings are listed in Deuteronomy 7:13-15, but before we look at them, I want to read this passage the way some Christians seem to think it reads: "And God will put sickness upon you. He will cause some of your children to be stillborn and some of them to die when they are babies. He will cause some of you to be sick and crippled all of your life."

That's the way some people portray God's character. But let's read what the Bible actually says.

> **DEUTERONOMY 7:13-15**
> 13 And he [God] will love thee, and bless thee, and multiply thee: he will also bless the fruit of thy womb, and the fruit of thy land, thy corn, and thy wine, and thine oil, the increase of thy kine, and the flocks of thy sheep, in the land which he sware unto thy fathers to give thee.
> 14 Thou shalt be blessed above all people: there shall not be male or female barren among you, or among your cattle.
> 15 And the Lord will take away from thee all sickness, and will put [permit] none of the evil diseases of Egypt, which thou knowest, upon thee. . . .

This promise is for us today, or God is not God. But if you still aren't convinced that these promises apply to us today, let's see what the *New* Testament has to say.

> **1 CORINTHIANS 10:11**
> 11 Now all these things happened unto them [Israel] for ensamples [examples or types]: and they are written for our admonition. . . .

> **1 CORINTHIANS 10:11 (*NIV*)**
> 11 These things happened to them as examples and were written down as warnings for us, on whom the fulfilment of the ages has come.

In this verse, Paul tells us the things that happened to Israel were written down as examples for us! What kind of things happened to Israel? Well, for one, in Exodus, God established a covenant of healing! Two, in Deuteronomy, the Lord said He would take away their sickness!

Just as the children of Israel had to stay under the Covenant in the Old Testament for God to be Jehovah

Rapha in their lives, so we have to stay under His covenant. It's real simple. Living in line with God's Word and doing what God said to do is how we remain under the covenant.

As I said, one thing the Word tells us is to love the Lord our God with all our heart, all our soul, and all our strength, and to love our neighbors as ourselves (Luke 10:27). The commandment of love actually sums up all the other commandments, because when we are walking in love, we won't steal, we won't lie, we won't kill, and so forth.

TAXES, TITHES, AND THE TRUTH

When we really love God, we won't steal from the government. Instead, we will do what the Bible says and "render unto Caesar that which is Caesar's, and render unto God that which is God's" (Matt. 22:21). This passage in Matthew 22 is talking about taxes. I know people who are born again and claim to be living for God, and they transact everything in cash so they won't have to pay any taxes. That is morally wrong. And one reason it's wrong is, the individual who doesn't pay taxes is making the rest of us law-abiding citizens pay his share while he has a free ride, so to speak.

Someone might ask, "What does paying taxes have to do with living under the covenant or with healing?" Well, the person who doesn't pay his share of taxes shouldn't expect to receive healing. Not obeying the government's authority and our civic laws means he isn't living right in the sight of God. It means he is a cheat and a fraud.

That may sound harsh, but this is where I shell down the corn, so to speak. This is where the rubber meets the road. We can't try to make things look right when they aren't right!

You see, many Christians who want healing, provision, and so forth, aren't living right! They say, "But I'm not doing this, that, and the other thing," referring to what mankind considers flagrant sins. There are many other things that are sin besides murder, adultery, and so forth. In fact, the Word of God says that stirring up strife among the brethren is a sin.

Remember, the Bible says that the Old Testament was written for our admonition. And Exodus 23:25 says if we will serve the Lord our God, He will bless our bread, and our water; He will take sickness away from our midst, and the number of our days He will fulfill. The condition is, we must diligently hearken to His voice. In other words, we must be careful to hear and do all that His Word says!

Many people want to grab hold of the faith message or a sermon on healing and run off with it without ever understanding the basic principles of God's Word. Well, we're not going to grab hold of faith and healing and run off with it until we understand the statutes and laws of God that He has put down in His Word. We are supposed to live by those statutes and laws!

One of those laws has to do with money—*m-o-n-e-y*. Tithing is a biblical principle. Ten percent of what we earn belongs to God, and if we aren't paying Him that much, then we are robbing Him (Mal. 3:8). That is what the Bible says. And if we are disobedient in any area, then we are not walking in His statutes, and there is no way He can manifest Himself in our life as the Lord that heals us.

When a person doesn't pay tithes, something will often go wrong with the car, the house, and so forth. And when you add the total expenses up, it would probably equal what the person's tithes should have been.

God doesn't cause things to go wrong in a person's life, but when you get out from under the Covenant, you give the enemy opportunity to come in and do it. For example, you might think you could save money by not tithing, but it will cost you money anyway. If a person will pay his tithes, the windows of Heaven will be opened on him to pour him out a blessing (Mal. 3:10). Now that doesn't necessarily mean he is going to get a thousand dollars next week, but if you will be faithful to God, He *will* bless you! Payday may not come every Friday, but it *will* come!

GOD'S HEALING COVENANT IS FOR TODAY!

Christians must realize and believe that the promise of healing is for us today. Jehovah Rapha is just as much for us today as He was for Israel in the Old Testament. Unfortunately, when some people hear about the blessings God provided for the children of Israel, they say, "But that was just in the Old Testament. Yes, Israel had Jehovah Rapha, Jehovah Nissi, and so forth. They were blessed by Jehovah, but we're not in the Old Testament. This is today!"

What makes anyone think that God's covenant in the Old Testament would be any greater than the covenant He made with the Church of His Son, Jesus Christ? I'm quite sure God the Father wants the Church to have it even better than Israel had it!

Someone might ask, "How can you be so sure that God is that way?" Because I know as a father I want my children to have it better than I had it. And I believe every father can say the same thing. Generally speaking, fathers want their children to have it better than they did. Well, the Bible says that God's ways are higher than ours (Isa. 55:9), so if we want good things for our natural children, how much more does our Heavenly Father want good things for us!

The blessings in the Old Testament included prosperity, health, healing, deliverance, salvation, and so forth.[1] God is still the same God He was in the Old Testament! His blessings weren't just for the children of Israel—the blessings are for His children today!

Many Christians sing the song that states, in effect, "Here we wander like a beggar through the heat and the cold." Friend, I am not a beggar, and I am not wandering! I'm a child of God under the covenant, and I'm blessed with the provisions of the covenant. I'm not wandering around; I'm on my way to Heaven. I'm "occupying"— serving Him—until He gets ready to call me in.

We should not tolerate sickness. Instead, when symptoms appear, we ought to command sickness to leave our body in the Name of Jesus. Every individual Christian is a member of the Body of Christ—the Church, the "ecclesia," which means the *called-out ones.* When we see another member of the Body sick and afflicted, we should stand our ground and say, "In the Name of Jesus, devil, you have no right to afflict *any* part of the Body of Christ."

Sometimes at healing crusades, I get upset when I see God's people suffering, because they don't have to suffer. Maybe they don't know about God's healing covenant, but I do! And I'm going to do what I can to help them get delivered.

That should be every Christian's attitude. We have a covenant with God that says, "He is our Healer!" We're not beggars. God provided so much for us when He provided salvation in His Son Jesus Christ.

Romans 1:16 says, *"For I am not ashamed of the gospel of Christ: for it is the power of God unto SALVATION. . . ."* Scofield's footnote on the word "salvation" states that the Greek and Hebrew imply the ideas of deliverance, safety, preservation, healing, and health (soundness). The Gospel of Jesus Christ, then, is the power of God unto deliverance, safety, preservation, healing, and health! In other words, when we are saved by the blood of the Lord Jesus Christ, we not only receive eternal life, but we also receive deliverance, safety, preservation, healing, and soundness. I didn't say we are *going to have* all those things. We already have them!

HEBREWS 8:6
6 But now hath he [Jesus] obtained a more excellent ministry, by how much also he is the mediator of a better covenant, which was established upon better promises.

This verse says we have a new and better covenant. Since it's new and better than the old, then it must contain all that was in the Old Covenant and *additional* promises; otherwise, it's not new or better. The Old Covenant, established between God and His man Abraham, provided healing for the children of Israel. And the New Covenant, purchased by the blood of the Lord Jesus Christ, was also established by Jehovah

Rapha, the Lord who heals us, and it provides healing
for the children of God.

LIVING UNDER THE UMBRELLA

The Book of Psalms was Israel's song and prayer
book. It is full of scriptures on healing, deliverance,
salvation, and the Lord's sustaining or preserving
power.

> **PSALM 103:3-5**
> **3 Who** [God] **forgiveth all thine iniquities; who
> healeth all thy diseases;**
> **4 Who redeemeth thy life from destruction; who
> crowneth thee with lovingkindness and tender
> mercies;**
> **5 Who satisfieth thy mouth with good things; so
> that thy youth is renewed like the eagle's.**

I am being renewed! I will never be old and decrepit,
because my youth is being renewed like the eagle's!

God's blessings and provisions are always available
to us. We partake of them by living according to God's
Word. The only time the children of Israel who lived
under the Old Covenant had problems was when they
didn't live according to God's covenant. Therefore, they
took themselves out from under the protection the covenant provided. God never left them; they left God.

You see, when we walk out from under the protection of the covenant, we open ourselves up to the devil's
attacks.

In the natural, if you walk out from underneath
an umbrella while it's raining, you're going to get wet.
Even if you carry an umbrella and have it opened while

it's raining, if you aren't underneath it, you will get wet! You can't just hold an opened umbrella and expect to stay dry. You have to stay underneath the opened umbrella.

You see, as Christians, we have an opened umbrella of protection, so to speak, called the blood covenant. But just knowing the covenant exists is like having an umbrella but never opening it. In other words, it doesn't do us a bit of good. And just using part of the covenant— walking in it sometimes and not walking in it at other times—is like having an opened umbrella but not standing under it. That, too, doesn't do us much good. Yet that is what many Christians are doing. They have the covenant, but they aren't walking in line with it, so it's not doing them any good. Then they wonder why they're sick, why they don't have any finances, and why everything is going wrong.

Friend, I want to stay as near to the protection of the covenant as I can. Have you ever noticed that when it's raining really hard, people with umbrellas will hold the umbrella handle so close to themselves that the handle is practically crushing their ribs. But the umbrella is protecting them, and they are staying dry!

That's what we need to do with the covenant of God—pull it in and get as close to it as we possibly can get. I'm not interested in how close I can walk to the edge and still be in the covenant. I want to get as far away from the edge as possible. I want to be living under the "spout where the blessing is coming out"!

God is still God. He is still Jehovah Rapha the Lord who heals us. We have a better covenant of healing than the children of Israel did in the Old Testament. Thank God for the Old Covenant, because all of it was included in the New Covenant when Jesus ratified it with His blood. But thank God for the New Covenant, of which we are benefactors in Christ!

We need to get hold of these foundational truths and walk in our healing covenant in a greater measure. As we move forward with God, we shall receive healing for ourselves and even for others as we share the news of the Covenant. We have a covenant with God Himself. He is our Healer!

---

[1]For an in-depth teaching on this subject, please *see Redeemed From the Curse of Poverty, Sickness, and Spiritual Death* by Kenneth E. Hagin.

CHAPTER 4

———

HEALING BELONGS TO YOU

As I stated in previous chapters, while this teaching on healing may seem elementary to some people, it is important to continually review what we already know in order to strengthen our faith. I may be reminding you of many things you already know, but sometimes we all need to be reminded.

Many times in church meetings and crusades, we have seen marvelous healings and miracles occur through manifestations of the Spirit. Unfortunately, many people get the idea in their head that they will just wait for a manifestation of the Spirit. But we can't always guarantee that God is going to move in some spectacular way, because the Word of God says that the gifts of the Spirit are manifested at the direction of the Spirit, as *He* wills, not as *we* will (1 Cor. 12:11). In other words, we can't work them up, and we can't make them happen. The spiritual gifts—including the gifts of healings, working of miracles, and the gift of faith—all happen as the Spirit of God wills.

What if we are expecting to receive healing through a manifestation of a gift of the Spirit, and it doesn't happen? What recourse do we have? We have *God's Word*. You see, we can't depend on a manifestation of a gift of the Spirit. But we can *always* depend on the Word, because the Word always works.

The Word works whether or not we feel like it does. God's Word works whether or not there is any immediate physical manifestation. And because the Word always works, the manifestation of the gifts of the Spirit do not have to be in operation for you to be healed. You can be healed though simple faith in God's Word.

Personally, I have seen just as many marvelous healings take place when no one laid hands on anyone or prayed for anyone. People simply received the Word of God by faith and got up from the bed of affliction, healed. There wasn't any spectacular sound of thunder. There wasn't a rushing mighty wind. In fact, at first there was no physical manifestation at all. People simply read God's Word, got hold of what God's Word had to say about divine healing, and received healing.

My father's healing testimony is one such testimony. He was healed simply by faith in the Word of God. He wasn't healed by a special manifestation of the gifts of the Spirit. In fact, he didn't even know about the gifts of the Spirit when he was healed. All he knew was God's Word. He read the Word, believed what it said, and was miraculously healed.

Some Christians think they have to go to a healing service and have hands laid on them in order to be healed. But we can be delivered from sickness and disease and have fantastic miracles take place in our life even if we are alone on a deserted island—because the Word of God works!

We need to learn what the Bible says about healing and learn how to exercise our faith in that Word, because exercising our faith in the Word of God brings the most marvelous results! Whether we realize it or not, God's Word is anointed. We can be spiritually dry, but when we start reading and meditating on the Word of God, suddenly something happens! We become refreshed and strengthened in our faith and it's because of the anointing.

Many Christians talk about wanting to attend a service where the anointing is flowing. Yes, it's the anointing that destroys the yoke, or bondage, that has people bound (Isa. 10:27). But we don't have to attend some special service to be where the anointing is flowing. When we have the Word of God, we have the anointing. The Word of God is anointed!

Certainly, there is such a thing as revival, and I thank God for the revival that is taking place in different parts of the world. But I can sit down in my house, begin to read the Word of God, and the same anointing that is in a revival meeting halfway across the country is in my very home, because the anointing is on God's Word.

Psalm 107:20 says, *"He* [God] *sent his word, and healed them, and delivered them from their destructions."* God's Word is anointed! His Word heals and delivers. And His Word is the same, whether or not we see any immediate manifestations.

Unfortunately, too many people wait for a manifestation of the gifts of the Spirit when they should simply get hold of the Word. Thank God, there is healing through the laying on of hands and through the gifts of the Spirit. But if Christians would just get hold of the Word, we wouldn't even have to have hands laid on us. We can get hold of God's Word and walk free from sickness—healed and made whole!

It's the Word that will set us free. And the Word says, *"Himself* took our infirmities, and bare our sicknesses; by whose stripes ye were healed" (Matt. 8:17; 1 Peter 2:24). Who is "Himself"? It is Jesus! And if we *were* healed, then we *are* healed! Since we are healed, why should we accept and put up with sickness?

Now I didn't say Christians won't ever have to fight a battle. But when the enemy comes against us, all we have to do is take the Word and overcome him by the blood of the Lamb and the word of our testimony (Rev. 12:11).

Again, the anointing is on God's Word. That's why in Second Timothy 4:2, Paul told Timothy to preach the Word. In churches today, we should still focus on preaching the Word. Unfortunately, many Christians depend on some program to increase church growth. Now don't misunderstand me. There is nothing wrong with church programs. But the Bible tells us to preach the Word! Of course, we don't need to be silly and ignore the things we can do in the natural to help our church. But when we preach the Word, God will confirm His Word, and people will come to church.

We preach the Word of God at RHEMA Bible Church, and since "RHEMA Praise" has been airing RHEMA Bible Church services on television, we have seen many people visit our church and get saved, delivered, and healed as a result. It is so important that we preach the Word!

It's through God's Word that we have assurance of our salvation. It's through the Word that we have assurance of our healing. It's through the Word that we have assurance of our prosperity. It's through the Word that we have assurance of eternal life. All the answers we need are in the Word!

Many Christians wouldn't need to be counseled or need as much counseling if they spent an hour praying and an hour reading the Word before they asked for counseling. Not very long ago, I preached at a church where the pastor had a standing counseling policy. The pastor told me, "Before I will counsel anyone, he or she has to come to the church for seven days and pray an hour each day. Most of the time I don't end up counseling anyone. They get counseling from the great Counselor."

GOD'S REDEMPTIVE PLAN INCLUDES HEALING

We know that it is God's will to heal. Healing is included in God's redemptive plan. Someone might say, "Everyone doesn't get healed." That's right. And everyone doesn't get saved, either. But, I'm not going to quit preaching salvation or healing just because someone didn't get saved or someone didn't get healed. I'm still going to preach Jesus saves; I'm still going to preach Jesus heals; and I'm still going to preach Jesus redeems!

Jesus wants to make us well! According to the Bible, Jesus Himself took our infirmities and bore our sicknesses (Matt. 8:17). Sickness and disease don't belong to us! They belong to the devil and come from him. Healing belongs to us!

The Greek word "sozo," which is sometimes translated "save" in the New Testament, is also translated "heal" in other New Testament passages. Just as Jesus purchased salvation for us through His death, burial, and resurrection, He also purchased healing for us!

WHAT YOU DON'T KNOW MIGHT HURT YOU

Unless we renew our minds by the Word of God, we won't realize that God is the Healer and Satan is the author of sickness and disease. That's one reason Paul tells us in Romans 12:2 to renew our mind. You see, our spirit becomes recreated when we are born again. God takes care of that. But we have the responsibility to do something with our mind. The problem is, many Christians never take the time to renew their mind. Instead, many just get hold of enough of God's Word to be dangerous to themselves and others. They are never in the Word enough to receive full knowledge—and partial knowledge can be dangerous.

Many years ago, when I was going to Bible school, I worked at a plastic manufacturing company in Dallas, Texas. My job was to run a bowl press—a little microwave-like machine that heated plastic pellets and melted them down to be pressed into shape within the mold. With special gloves on, I would take three pellets in each hand, put them in the mold, and push a button to close the press.

When the mold came down on top of the melted pellets, the soft plastic would be pressed into the shape of a bowl. The inside of that mold was operated at 350 degrees Fahrenheit, a temperature which would burn a person very quickly! In fact, even though I wore special gloves, sometimes the back of my hands would still be red eight hours after having my hands in that heat. There were certain ways to operate the press machine, and all the workers were taught the proper methods. If we didn't operate the machine according to those methods, we could get hurt.

One night, a new guy was working on my shift, and I was trying to train him properly. I told him, "You do it methodically, or you're going to get hurt."

He brushed off my instructions and said, "Oh, I know what to do. This is easy."

He didn't even make one eight-hour shift without having to go to the hospital. The foreman reprimanded me and said, "Hagin, I thought I told you to train him."

I said, "I did! I told him everything, and I told him to be methodical. But he said, 'Oh, just let me do it. This is easy.'"

The foreman asked me, "How long did he let you train him?" I answered, "Probably five minutes."

You see, that young man fresh on the job received just enough knowledge to get himself in trouble. He almost lost an arm, because he only had partial knowledge on how to operate that machine. A similar thing can happen when it comes to Christians and the Word of God. Many times, after a person becomes a Christian, he begins to receive *partial* knowledge about all that God wants to bless him with, such as healing, prosperity, and so forth. But he runs off with what little he knows and gets himself in trouble. Then he may want to blame God when things don't work out the way he thought they are supposed to.

CHILDREN OF A BETTER COVENANT

We need to renew our mind to the fact that Satan is the author of sickness, disease, and everything that is evil. Then we will be able to clearly understand what God's Word says. And we will also see what Jesus does and what Satan does.

People can take any teaching to the extreme. But the truth is that God wants to bless His children. Throughout the Word of God, we read that God wants to bless. He blessed Abraham. How did He bless him? God blessed Abraham with spiritual, physical, and financial blessings.

Many years ago, there was a popular song we used to sing that said, "Abraham's blessings are mine." And it's true! According to the Word of God, Abraham's blessings are mine! And they are yours, too, if you are a child of God.

> **LUKE 13:11-16**
> 11 And, behold, there was a woman which had a spirit of infirmity eighteen years, and was bowed together, and could in no wise lift up herself.
> 12 And when Jesus saw her, he called her to him, ånd said unto her, Woman, thou art loosed from thine infirmity [Notice, Jesus told her she was loosed before He ever laid hands on her or did anything.].
> 13 And he laid his hands on her: and immediately she was made straight, and glorified God.
> 14 And the ruler of the synagogue answered with indignation, because that Jesus had healed on the sabbath day, and said unto the people, There are six days in which men ought to work: in them therefore come and be healed, and not on the sabbath day.
> 15 The Lord then answered him, and said, Thou hypocrite, doth not each one of you on the sabbath loose his ox or his ass from the stall, and lead him away to watering?
> 16 And ought not this woman, BEING A DAUGHTER OF ABRAHAM, whom Satan hath bound, lo, these eighteen years, be loosed from this bond on the sabbath day?

First, notice where the spirit of infirmity came from. Verse 16 says, "Whom *Satan* hath bound." This is just more scriptural proof that sickness and disease come from the devil!

Jesus declared that the woman ought to be loosed for two reasons. The first reason was that Satan had her bound. You see, all sickness, disease, and bondage are from Satan. God's people shouldn't be bound by anything. Just as one song says, "We don't have to be sick no more; don't have to be poor no more; don't have to be bound no more—by *anything*!"

Jesus paid the price to set us free from Satan's bondage. He took our sickness to the Cross, just as surely as He took our sin. We need to get hold of that fact. Mankind's sickness and disease went to the Cross just as our sins went to the Cross. The benefits of Redemption were all tied together in one package, and we can't have one part of it without the other! Many people try to take just one part of the package. Many Christians talk about salvation but won't talk about healing. However, salvation and healing come together; we can't separate them!

Jesus gave a second reason the woman should be healed. He said it was that she was a daughter of Abraham. Someone might say, "That was under the Old Covenant, so it isn't for us today." Well, friend, Hebrews 8:6 says, *"But now hath he [Jesus] obtained a more excellent ministry, by how much also he is the mediator of a BETTER covenant, which was established upon BETTER promises."* As Christians, we have a better covenant! And since it's a *better* covenant, then we know it includes all the promises that were in the Old Covenant—and then some!

Some Christians try to argue that the woman in Luke 13 was healed because she was a daughter of

Abraham, and, since we're not related to Abraham, it doesn't apply to us. But the Book of Galatians tells us that we are Abraham's seed!

> **GALATIANS 3:29**
> **29 And if ye be Christ's, then are ye ABRAHAM'S SEED, and heirs according to the promise.**

What was the promise? Redemption from the curse of the Law! Redemption from spiritual death! Redemption from poverty! And redemption from sickness and disease! What a wonderful promise!

Galatians 3:29 says, "If you are Christ's." If you are a Christian, then you are Christ's. And if you are Christ's, then, according to God's Word, you are Abraham's seed. And if you are Abraham's seed, you are an heir according to the promise.

> **GALATIANS 3:7**
> **7 Know ye therefore that they which are of faith, the same are the children of Abraham.**

As I said, the second reason Jesus gave explaining why the woman should be loosed was that she was a daughter of Abraham. Paul said in Galatians that through the blood of the Lord Jesus Christ, we have been adopted and engrafted into the family, making us children of Abraham. If we are children of Abraham, then we are sons and daughters. And if that daughter of Abraham in the New Testament shouldn't be sick, then a daughter of Abraham *today* shouldn't be sick!

Jesus gave two reasons why the woman in Luke chapter 13 shouldn't be sick and ought to be loosed. Those two reasons are the same reasons why *we* shouldn't be sick, down, depressed, defeated, poor, or in bondage to anything. Number one, any type of bondage is of Satan. And, number two, we are children of Abraham through Christ Jesus!

Again, there are two reasons why we *can* and *ought to* be free. Bondage is of Satan, and Jesus said that those in Christ ought to be loosed. Second, if we are in Christ, we are Abraham's seed and heirs according to the promise. We are sons and daughters of the Most High God, and healing belongs to us!

If you are sick in your body today, receive the Word that I have shared with you in this chapter. You don't have to read any further in this book to be healed. You can believe and receive right now! Just reach up, so to speak, by faith, and take hold of what belongs to you. You're a child of God, Abraham's seed, and a son or daughter of the promise. Healing belongs to you!

CHAPTER 5

TWO METHODS OF RECEIVING HEALING

Even though most of the teaching we have studied so far covers the basic truths about healing, they are vitally important truths. And I am covering the basics in a little different way than maybe has been done before. I want to make the subject of healing very simple so that people can easily understand it. It is what you personally know about God's Word that will benefit you.

Many Christians take a subject in the Bible and generalize it. The subject of prayer is one such subject. You see, there are many different types or methods of prayer taught in the Bible, but Christians tend to throw them all together in one sack, so to speak, and shake it up. All of it is still considered "prayer," but we need to recognize and understand the different types of prayer so we will be able to put the right prayer method with what we want to communicate to God or to receive from Him.

Some Christians have done the same thing with the subject of healing as they have with prayer. They've put everything into one sack and mixed it all up together. But, you see, there are many different methods of receiving healing mentioned in the Bible. Biblical methods for receiving healing include the laying on of hands, the Name of Jesus, and simple faith in the Word of God.

There are many different biblical methods whereby we can receive healing, but in this chapter, I want to study two of the ways we can receive healing from God.

JAMES 5:14-16
14 Is any sick among you? let him call for the
ELDERS of the church; and let them pray over him,
anointing him with oil in the name of the Lord:
15 And the prayer of faith shall save the sick, and
the Lord shall raise him up; and if he have committed sins, they shall be forgiven him.
16 Confess your faults one to another, and pray one
for another, that ye may be healed. The effectual
fervent prayer of a righteous man availeth much.

MARK 5:25-30,34
25 And a certain woman, which had an issue of
blood twelve years,
26 And had suffered many things of many physi-
cians, and had spent all that she had, and was
nothing bettered, but rather grew worse,
27 When she had heard of Jesus, came in the press
behind, and touched his garment.
28 For she said, If I may touch but his clothes, I
shall be whole.
29 And straightway the fountain of her blood was
dried up; and she felt in her body that she was
healed of that plague.
30 And Jesus, immediately knowing in himself
that virtue [power or anointing] had gone out of
him, turned him about in the press, and said, Who
touched my clothes? . . .
34 And he said unto her, Daughter, thy faith hath
made thee whole; go in peace, and be whole of thy
plague.

I want you to notice two things from these passages
of Scripture. Number one, we learn from James 5:14
that a person may be healed when the elders of the
church pray over him. And, number two, we learn from
Mark chapter 5 that the woman with the issue of blood
was healed when the anointing flowed out from Jesus

and into her body. Both methods produced the same results—healing.

James 5:14 uses the word "elders." In the Bible, and especially in the New Testament, the terms "elder," "bishop," and "overseer" mean *pastor*. James is talking about calling for the pastor. Also, James 5:14, which states, *"Is there any sick among you? let him call for the elders of the church . . ."* includes those who are shut-in and can't go to church services.

One way to receive healing, and the first of two ways we will study in this chapter, is through prayer. We can either pray for ourself or have someone else pray for us.

Mark 11:24 says, *". . .What things soever ye desire, when ye pray, believe that ye receive them, and ye shall have them."* The phrase "what things soever" in this verse includes healing. If it didn't include healing, the verse would have said, "Whatsoever things you desire *except healing*, believe that you receive them, and you shall have them." And the phrase "when you pray" indicates that the person desiring healing for himself is doing the praying. You see, we can call for the elders to come and pray for us, or we can pray the prayer ourself.

When I was fifteen years old, I had an ear problem that persisted over a long period of time. My dad prayed for me, and my pastor prayed for me, but I didn't get healed. Finally, my dad told me that he had prayed about the situation and God told him that I had to pray for my healing myself.

You see, I had been taught the Bible, and I knew enough about the healing power of God that I needed to do my own praying. But when my dad and I knelt down to pray, I didn't say anything. I just waited for him to do the praying.

After a few moments of silence, I finally asked him, "Are you going to pray?"

He said, "No, I'm not going to pray. I don't need anything. You are the one who needs something, so *you* pray! I'm just here to agree with you. I'm here to 'scotch' your prayer."

Let me explain what "scotch your prayer" means. It's a phrase we used to use back where I come from when a car was parked on a hill, for example, and needed support to keep it from rolling. We used to say, "Scotch the wheels with something so the car doesn't roll." "Scotch the wheels" meant to put a rock, brick, or something similar behind and under the rear wheel to keep the car from rolling.

So when my dad and I knelt together to pray for my ear, my dad was there to "scotch my prayer" or to simply back me up and give me support in case I needed it.

But I prayed for myself to receive healing for my ear, and I was healed after I prayed that prayer. In fact, when my hearing was tested, I was told that the ear I had prayed for was a lot stronger than the ear that hadn't been affected. And the ear that was supposed to be permanently damaged from the disease is still working perfectly today!

HEALING IS FOR EVERYONE

When James wrote, asking, "Is there any sick among you?" he was writing to believers (James 5:14). He asked if there were *any* sick, which tells us that sickness wasn't expected or assumed to be a common occurrence among Christians. It also tells us that if there *were* any sick, there couldn't have been very many; otherwise James wouldn't have asked if there was *any*. Unfortunately, if James were writing to believers today to tell them how to be healed, he would have to say, "The *ninety percent* of you who are sick. . . ." Evidently, there weren't that many sick people in the Early Church. And the reason is simple—believers in the Early Church understood how to receive their healing.

In fact, until the close of the sixth century, believers generally believed that healing was always God's will and that sickness and disease were satanic oppression and should be cured in every case by means of prayer and by invoking the Name of Jesus. However, with the advent of the reign of Pope Gregory I in A.D. 590, the pure message of divine healing began to be obscured by Gregory's belief that sickness and disease were one of the ways God chastised His children. Gregory considered sickness to be the scourge of God's discipline and wrath instead of the result of satanic oppression. As Gregory's teachings gained popularity, sickness was no longer widely regarded as the work of the enemy, nor was it any longer thought that the sick should be healed in every instance.[1]

But the Bible teaches us that healing is God's will for everyone—every time! You see, James 5:14 says, "If *any one* of you is sick . . . ," proving that healing is for everyone. Unfortunately, some people today are trying to teach that healing is only for a special group of people. They teach that an individual must be a "good Christian" for a number of years in order to be a candidate for healing. People who espouse this belief do so because of wrong thinking or wrong teaching.

In years gone by, even some in Pentecostal churches taught along these lines—so much so that it tended to make some of the older church members mad when someone just got saved and received healing. Some people said, "God, I've been saved all these years, and I've done such-and-such in the church for years. Yet You healed that individual who only got saved last week!"

You see, according to the Bible, healing is not *merited*. We don't *earn* healing by performing a certain number of Christian tasks. Healing is for everyone just as salvation is for everyone. Remember, one reason we know healing is for everyone is because James asked, "Is *any* sick among you?" James didn't make any exceptions or qualifications; his instructions on how to be healed were for *anyone* who was sick!

James didn't just tell the believers they *could* be healed, he told them what they must do *to be* healed! *Number one*, they were to call for the elders of the church. Remember, we are to call for the elders to come to us if we are shut-in and have no way to attend a service on our own. Otherwise, we are to go to church or where a service is being held and have the elders pray for us there.

Number two, James said the elders were to anoint the sick one with oil and pray the prayer of faith. One way to receive healing is to call for the elders of the church, who will anoint the sick with oil and pray. And the Bible says that the prayer of faith shall save the sick!

We've learned in previous chapters that the word "save" is from the Greek word "sozo." In some places in the New Testament, sozo is translated "saved," and in other places, it's translated "healed." And according to the *Scofield Reference Bible*, the word "sozo" implies the ideas of salvation, healing, preservation, and deliverance.

So, according to the meaning of the original Greek, we can read James 5:15, "And the prayer of faith shall *heal* the sick," because that is what it means!

The only time "save" might be okay to use is when a person who is shut-in due to a terminal illness calls for the elders to come anoint him with oil and pray for him. Then the word "saved" might be a good word to use, because through the prayer of faith, he can be healed of the terminal illness, which means his life would be saved. As we saw earlier in this chapter, the implication in James' instructions for calling on the elders for prayer is that those who called for the elders were so sick that it was impossible for them to get to the meetings. That meant that those who called for the elders were so sick that they may have been dying, which would explain why translators used the word "save" instead of "heal."

There are different methods of prayer, and, thank God, each method works! For example, an individual who has faith in God and His Word can simply pray for himself and be healed. Or he can call for the elders of the church to come pray for him. Or he can have other believers pray for him because the Bible says believers can pray one for another. Remember, James 5:16 says, ". . . *pray one for another, that ye may be HEALED. The effectual fervent prayer of a righteous man availeth much.*"

I like the way the latter part of that verse reads in *The Amplified Bible*: " . . . *The earnest (heartfelt, continued) prayer of a righteous man makes tremendous power available [dynamic in its working].*"

Someone might say, "But that verse is talking about a *righteous* man."

Well, if a person is born again, he *is* righteous or in right-standing with God. You see, many people confuse righteousness with spiritual growth or maturity. They confuse "righteousness" and "sanctification." Sanctification is a progressive work in a Christian's life. As we live for God each day, we become more and more in tune to the things of God, and, thereby, more and more sanctified by His Word.

But, although sanctification is a progressive work, righteousness is a one-time act! When someone is born again by the blood of Jesus Christ, he is instantly *made* to be in right-standing with God.

Righteousness comes from being in right-standing with God. And you become righteous the minute you are born again, cleansed by the blood of Jesus Christ and made a new creature in Christ. Second Corinthians 5:21 says, *"For he* [God] *hath made him* [Jesus] *to be sin for us, who knew no sin; that we might be made the RIGHTEOUSNESS OF GOD in him."* Whoever has been born again has been made righteous and can say, "I am the righteousness of God in Christ."

PRAYER MAKES POWER AVAILABLE

Remember, James 5:16 says, ". . . *The earnest (heartfelt, continued) prayer of a righteous man makes tremendous power available [dynamic in its working]"* (*Amplified*). I like the word "dynamic," but words just aren't adequate when it comes to describing the power of God that is made available through prayer!

As we pray, the healing power of God produces a manifestation of healing in our body. Remember, we can pray for ourselves or have the elders anoint us with oil and pray; the power of God is simply made available through the prayer of faith.

Some people say, "Well, you have to use 'anointing' oil or it won't work."

In the Old Testament, there were specific instructions on how to make the anointing oil. But the New Testament does not give us any specific instructions concerning the oil. Many Christians have taken oil to Jerusalem, and they have prayed over it in the tomb that is thought to be the tomb in which Jesus was buried. Those people think that doing such a thing is going to make the oil better to use. But the power of God is not any stronger in the tomb in Jerusalem than it is in your own house or wherever *you* are, because *you* are the tabernacle of the power of God! You are the tabernacle of the power of God, because Jesus lives in you. And the power of God is wherever God is!

Some Christians say, "Let's go to church and get blessed." But we should say, "Let's go to church and *be* a blessing," because we have the blessing in us! Wherever we go, we carry the blessing.

Some people think they have to go to Israel and get water from the Jordan River in order to be healed. They think that because Naaman dipped seven times in the Jordan River (2 Kings 5:14), that the water from the Jordan has some kind of healing power in it. Some so-called preachers even advertise, "Send me such-and-such amount of money as an offering, and I will send you some water from the Jordan River. If you rub it on your body, you will be healed."

That kind of promise just isn't scriptural. There may have been countless other people in the Jordan River at the same time Naaman dipped himself in the water, but none of them were healed. So why was Naaman healed by dipping in the water? Naaman was healed because he was obeying God.

We have examples in the New Testament in which obedience brought the blessing. In John chapter 9, Jesus told the blind man to go wash the mud off of his eyes at the pool of Siloam. When the man obeyed Jesus, he was healed (John 9:7)! You see, obedience to Jesus is obedience to the Word of God, because Jesus is the Living Word. The Bible says that Jesus is the Word made flesh (John 1:1,14).

There could have been other people besides the blind man washing their faces at the pool of Siloam, but nothing happened to them. The blind man's healing was a special manifestation of the power of God. Jesus put mud on the man's eyes, and the man went and washed it off as Jesus commanded him. What happened when the man obeyed the Word? He was healed!

THE HEALING ANOINTING

We are studying two different methods of receiving healing. We have looked at prayer and have covered different ways believers can receive healing through prayer. Now I want to deal with prayer in conjunction with the healing anointing.

A second method whereby we can receive healing is through the tangible anointing, or the healing power of God.[2] We see an example of a woman being healed by this method in Mark chapter 5. Starting in verse 30, the woman with the issue of blood has just touched Jesus' garment.

> **MARK 5:25-30,34**
> **25 And a certain woman, which had an issue of blood twelve years,**
> **26 And had suffered many things of many physicians,**

and had spent all that she had, and was nothing bettered, but rather grew worse,
27 When she had heard of Jesus, came in the press behind, and touched his garment.
28 For she said, If I may touch but his clothes, I shall be whole.
29 And straightway the fountain of her blood was dried up; and she felt in her body that she was healed of that plague.
30 And Jesus, immediately knowing in himself that virtue [The word "virtue" means power or anointing. The Greek word for virtue is "dunamis," from which we get our English word "dynamite."] **had gone out of him, turned him about in the press, and said, Who touched my clothes? . . .**
34 And he said unto her, Daughter, thy faith hath made thee whole; go in peace, and be whole of thy plague.

Notice that Jesus didn't tell this woman anything. He didn't tell her to go wash as He had told the blind man with the mud on his eyes to go wash. He didn't say, "Get up, take up your bed and walk" as He told the man taken with palsy in Luke chapter 5. And Jesus didn't touch her as He'd done with so many others in ministering healing. Many times in the Bible, Jesus gave the sick person a command, and when the sick one obeyed the command, he was healed. But, Jesus didn't even know this lady with the issue of blood was around when she received the healing anointing! If He had known, He wouldn't have had to ask, "Who touched Me?"

In this chapter, we have studied how to receive healing through prayer. In Jesus' ministry, He used many different methods to minister healing, but He primarily ministered with the anointing. And, most of the time, He ministered the anointing in connection with the laying on of hands.

How was Jesus able to heal? He was able to heal because He was anointed! Who anointed Him? God did. What was He anointed with? Remember, Acts 10:38, which says, *"How GOD ANOINTED Jesus of Nazareth WITH THE HOLY GHOST AND WITH POWER: who went about doing good, and healing all that were oppressed of the devil; for God was with him."*

Although Jesus primarily ministered with the anointing in connection with the laying on of hands, there are two places in the Bible where we read about people being healed by the anointing simply by touching Jesus' clothes. The woman with the issue of blood in Mark chapter 5 is one such example. The other is in Matthew chapter 14.

> **MATTHEW 14:34-36 (NIV)**
> 34 When they had crossed over, they landed at Gennesaret.
> 35 And when the men of that place recognized Jesus, they sent word to all the surrounding country. People brought all their sick to him
> 36 and begged him to let the sick just touch the edge of his cloak, and all who touched him were healed.

In some places in the New Testament, people went to Jesus wanting Him to touch them. In fact, sometimes they even said, "Put Your hand on me." But in Matthew 14:36, the people simply begged Jesus to let them touch His garment as He went by. Jesus didn't lay hands on them. They simply touched His garment, and the anointing was so strong that they were healed.

In Second Kings chapter 13, we find an example of the anointing being so strong that it brought the dead back to life!

2 KINGS 13:20,21

20 And Elisha died, and they buried him. And the bands of the Moabites invaded the land at the coming in of the year.

21 And it came to pass, as they were burying a man, that, behold, they spied a band of men; and they cast the man into the sepulchre of Elisha: and when the man was let down, and touched the bones of Elisha, he revived, and stood up on his feet.

In Second Kings chapter 2, the prophet Elisha had received a double portion of the anointing that was upon the prophet Elijah (v. 9). In Second Kings chapter 13, Elisha had already died and was buried. As the Moabites were burying a man killed in battle, they saw the enemy coming, so they threw the dead man in Elisha's grave—they threw him on the prophet Elisha's bones! And there was still enough residue of anointing left in Elisha's bones to cause the dead man to come alive!

That's the power of the anointing! And in Mark chapter 5, the woman with the issue of blood came in contact with that anointing. When she touched Jesus, He said, "Virtue has gone out of Me." He turned around and asked, "Who touched My clothes?" You see, Jesus knew that power had gone out of Him.

In the early part of my ministry, when I prayed for people to be healed, I anointed them with oil. But then God dealt with me especially to minister to the sick with a tangible anointing of the healing power of God. Now when I am ministering to the sick, as I lay hands on people, I can feel that anointing go out of me into them.

Sometimes the anointing ministered is stronger than at other times, and that has a lot to do with the sick person's faith. Sometimes when the anointing is ministered to someone, he doesn't receive or *keep* the anointing. You see, unless a person receives and keeps the anointing, it doesn't do him any good, and he doesn't receive anything.

Once I ministered to a sick woman along this line. Ms. M____ had faith to be free from pain, but she didn't have faith for healing. I talked to her about it several times, and she said, "I believe the pain will leave when you pray." She would call me at home some nights to pray for her over the phone, because that was the only way she could sleep. My wife can testify that some nights the phone rang every two to three hours. I would pray, and, according to her family, she would go right to sleep and be pain-free for two or three hours.

I tried my best to get her to take the same faith she used to receive relief from pain and use it to receive complete healing. I told her, "You can use the same faith, and the same anointing that stops the pain will completely heal you."

She said, "Well, yes, I guess it would, but I just don't have faith for that. But I can believe that if you will pray, the pain will go away."

My wife can testify that I did everything I could to help her. Although she believed that if I would pray, the anointing would take her pain away, she couldn't believe for the anointing to free her of her sickness. I tried to get the truth across to her, but I'm sorry to say that her sickness killed her. Thank God, she went on to Glory and she is with Jesus now. And I'm glad she was able to appropriate the power of God, which was made available through our prayers, to remain relatively free of pain while she was still on earth. But that wasn't God's best for her!

Remember, I had prayed for her over the telephone that she would be released of her pain. Notice, I didn't go lay hands on her each time she called. We simply prayed over the telephone. I didn't even anoint her with oil. We just prayed, and the anointing took away the pain. The anointing did it. It is important for you to understand that there is a connection between the anointing, or the healing power of God, and a person's faith.

THE ANOINTING DESTROYS THE YOKE!

According to Isaiah 10:27, it is the anointing that destroys the yoke of sickness and disease. Where does the anointing come from? It comes from God! What activates the anointing? *Faith gives action to the power!*

Now let's take a closer look at the story of the woman with the issue of blood and discover the connection between faith and the anointing.

> **MARK 5:30-34**
> **30 And Jesus, immediately knowing in himself that virtue had gone out of him, turned him about in the press, and said, Who touched my clothes?**
> **31 And his disciples said unto him, Thou seest the multitude thronging thee, and sayest thou, Who touched me?**
> **32 And he looked round about to see her that had done this thing.**
> **33 But the woman fearing and trembling, knowing what was done in her, came and fell down before him, and told him all the truth.**
> **34 And he said unto her, Daughter, THY FAITH hath made thee whole; go in peace, and be whole of thy plague.**

Reading Mark chapter 5, we know that other people touched Jesus that day and didn't get healed. Someone might say, "How do you know that other people touched Him?" Well, when Jesus asked the disciples, "Who touched Me?" the disciples said, "What are You talking about? Why are You saying, 'Who touched Me?' when this crowd is all around You?" In other words, in modern language, the disciples said, "Jesus, why do You ask 'Who touched Me?' when there is a crowd of people all around You? *Everyone* has been bumping up against You and touching You."

But, in effect, Jesus had said, "No, wait a minute. This is different. Power went out of Me."

Why didn't power go out from Him into the other people who may have stumbled, reached out, and put their hands on Jesus? Power didn't flow out from Him because there was no faith involved. The woman with the issue of blood had said, "If I can touch His clothes, I'll be whole," and the anointing flowed out of Jesus into her. Why? The anointing flows *to faith.*

In the natural, lamps or light bulbs do not operate until a switch is thrown and electricity flows through the wires into the bulb. When we flip the switch, contact is made. When contact is made, it allows the electricity to flow through a wire to the elements in that bulb, and we have light. Now that is a simplistic way of explaining electricity. I'm no electrician, but I know a little bit about how electricity works.

Anyone who turns a light switch on, takes the bulb out, and sticks his finger in the socket is going to get shocked, because he's going to make direct contact with the power of electricity! But he can turn the light switch *off*, which will stop the electrical current from flowing into the lamp, take out the bulb, and stick his finger in the socket all he wants to—and nothing will happen.

Our faith is like a light switch. When we turn the switch on, it allows the power of God—the anointing—to flow. We need to look at our faith as being the switch that turns on, or activates, the power of God.

One winter day, it was cold inside my house, so I had the heat on. But then the temperature got up into the 60s, and the house started warming up. With the sun shining in, the temperature got a lot warmer than I wanted it to be. The switch on my thermostat which reads "cool" and "heat" was turned to the "heat" side. But when I flipped that little switch to where it read "cool," I immediately heard the compressor and fan turn on, and I felt cool air blowing out of the vents. That air-conditioning unit's power to cool was present and available all the time. But the cooling power laid dormant, so to speak, until I turned the switch and made contact with it.

Nothing happened with that cooling power until I made contact with it. And that is the same principle we need to understand about the anointing. The anointing is present all the time. The power of God to heal is always *present*, but it is not in *manifestation* until contact is made with it.

You see, the anointing is always present to heal, but it lies dormant until someone makes contact with it by faith. A minister could lay hands on a sick person until he wore every hair off the top of the sick person's head. But that person won't receive anything until he turns on the switch of faith and receives the anointing.

In the past, after my wife and I have prayed for people in a healing line, my wife has said, "I feel so bad about So-and-so. He didn't receive healing."

I told her, "I don't know which person you're talk-ing about, but I know there were about five people I touched, and when I did, it was as though the anointing was short-circuited."

You see, when the anointing is flowing and I lay hands on someone who isn't in faith, the anointing isn't effectual. To explain it in natural terms, it's similar to having a short circuit. When the switch of faith isn't turned on, it "short-circuits" the anointing. In fact, many times after I have laid hands on about four or five people in a row who are not in faith, it so affects the anointing that it takes three to five people who are in faith before the anointing comes back strong again.

Now someone might ask, "Why does it work that way?" I don't know why it works that way. But I've talked to various ministers, including my father, Rev. Kenneth E. Hagin, who minister healing that way, and they all have told me the same thing happens to them!

It was only after the Holy Ghost had come upon Jesus that He had this power to minister healing. Jesus received the anointing when the Holy Ghost came upon Him as a dove (Luke 3:22). Up until that time, there were no miracles recorded. It was only after ". . . *God anointed Jesus of Nazareth with the Holy Ghost and with power . . .*" that Jesus began to heal and work miracles (Acts 10:38).

God has a role to play, and the person who needs healing has a role to play. You see, when the tangible anointing is administered to an individual, the power of God is present to heal. But if that person does not turn on the switch of faith to receive the anointing, nothing will happen!

In Mark 5:34, Jesus said to the woman with the issue of blood, *". . . Daughter, THY FAITH hath made thee whole. . . ."* Notice Jesus didn't say, *"My power* has made you whole," because something else besides God's power was involved—the woman's faith! You see, God's power, His anointing, is always available to anyone who will activate it by turning on the switch of faith.

Someone might say, "I thought it was the anointing that healed her."

Yes, the anointing had a part to play in it, but it was the woman's *faith* that caused the anointing to work on her behalf!

In this chapter, we have studied two scriptural methods for receiving healing. The first method is prayer. It can be prayer by the elders, prayer for one's self, or prayer one for another. The second method is receiving healing through the transference of the tangible healing power of God by the laying on of hands.

Anyone can receive healing at *any* time. We don't have to wait for someone who is specially anointed to pray for us, nor do we have to wait for the healing power to be manifested. We don't have to wait for the elders to pray for us, because we can pray for ourself, and we can pray one for another. It's the *anointing* that destroys the yoke, and God has made His anointing available to us so that we can receive divine healing.

---

[1]For a more detailed study of this subject, please *see* Kenneth W. Hagin's book *Healing: Forever Settled*.

[2]For a more detailed study of this subject, please *see* Kenneth E. Hagin's book *The Healing Anointing*.

CHAPTER 6

GOD'S WORD IS MEDICINE

In the previous chapter, we discussed how to receive healing through the anointing. We know we can receive healing through a manifestation of the gifts of the Spirit or through the healing power of God that is made available to us in a number of ways—through the laying on of hands and so forth. But God wants us to understand that there is also life and power in His Word! *God's Word is the never-failing remedy for whatever you need.* Whether it's sickness, disease, or financial difficulty that comes your way in life, God's Word is the answer for you!

> **PROVERBS 4:20-22**
> **20 My son, attend to my words; incline thine ear unto my sayings.**
> **21 Let them not depart from thine eyes; keep them in the midst of thine heart.**
> **22 For they** [God's words] **are life unto those that find them, and HEALTH TO ALL THEIR FLESH.**

According to this passage of Scripture, what is health to all man's flesh? God's words are! Does this passage say, "Attend to My words . . . for they are health unto your *spirit*"? No! It says God's Word is health to your *flesh*!

You see, God is as interested in our flesh as He is in our spirit. He wants His Spirit dwelling in a body that is healthy and whole, because He wants what is on the inside (His Spirit) to be demonstrated or manifested on the outside.

In John 6:63, Jesus tells us that God's Word is full of life—it's full of healing, health, and happiness. It's full of whatever you need at any given moment. God's Word is where your answer is!

JOHN 6:63
63. . .the words that I [Jesus] speak unto you, they are spirit, and they are life.

I thank God for all of the jumping and shouting Christians sometimes do in church services, and I'm as guilty as anyone of rejoicing during a service. I think it's fine to rejoice when the Spirit is moving in that way, but sometimes if we're not careful, we will begin to have wrong thinking about the moving of the Spirit or the manifestation of God's power. We will begin to think that a physical demonstration of some sort is a sign of God's power rather than understanding that God's Word contains more power than jumping, shouting, or any other physical demonstration does. God's power is in His Word!

Have you ever noticed how much power there is just in the Name of Jesus? Just saying, "Jesus, Jesus, Jesus" can stir up the power of God. I can't say the Name of Jesus very many times before my spirit starts doing "hand springs"! There is power in the Name of Jesus, and there is power in the Word of God.

Not only does God's Word contain *power*, but it contains *life*. You see, the Word of God is like medicine to our body! What happens when a person takes medicine? The medicine heals his body! We need to learn how to take the medicine of the Word of God and let it heal our body.

Let's take a closer look at Proverbs 4:20-22.

PROVERBS 4:20-22
20 My son, ATTEND to my words; INCLINE THINE EAR unto my sayings.
21 LET THEM NOT DEPART from thine eyes; KEEP THEM in the midst of thine heart.
22 For they are life unto those that find them, and health to all their flesh.

The word "attend" in verse 20 means *to give one's undivided attention*. This verse could be better understood if we read it like this: "Give your undivided attention to the words of God." When someone says, "I want your undivided attention," we know that means we're not supposed to be thinking about anything else, looking at anything else, or doing anything else, but we're supposed to focus directly on what that person is saying to us.

Almost everyone, at one time or another, has been in a classroom where the teacher has said, "I want all eyes on me. I want your undivided attention." When the teacher said that, it meant that the students weren't supposed to look out the window to see what was going on. It meant the boys weren't supposed to look and see if the girls were still as pretty as they were the last time they looked! No one was supposed to do anything except look at the teacher. Everyone was supposed to shut out all other thoughts and all other conversations and listen strictly to what the teacher had to say.

And that is exactly what God wants us to do! He wants us to shut out everything around us, and without any interruptions, give our undivided attention to His

Word! That is what the phrase "attend to My words" in Proverbs 4:20 tells us.

OPEN YOUR EARS!

The second part of Proverbs 4:20 states, "Incline your ear to My sayings." The word "incline" simply means *to listen*. Again, we could better understand verse 20 if we read it this way: "Listen with your ears to what I am saying." God is telling us to open up our ears to what He is saying.

It's interesting to note that a person can have perfect hearing, but if he decides he doesn't want to listen to someone who's talking, he can cut them off, so to speak. In other words, the sound of someone talking goes in his ear, but he doesn't really hear what that person says.

Many people do this when they're watching television and a commercial comes on. We can sit in front of the TV and hear sounds but never really hear what the commercial says because we fix our attention on or start thinking about something else.

For example, during a football game men sit in front of the TV and pay attention when the game is on. But when a commercial comes on, they turn their attention elsewhere until the football game comes back on, and then they tune right back in. Unfortunately, husbands can also use this skill when their wives are talking. You see, a husband can appear to be listening to his wife while she is talking but really be "tuning her out."

We shouldn't tune out God's Word. We need to open up our ears. In opening up our ears to His Word, we are closing our ears to everything contrary to what God is saying. So many times we are listening to what God says but we're also listening to what So-and-so says. We begin listening to this person and that person, this preacher and that preacher. But it doesn't make any difference what the preacher or Sister So-and-so says. What matters is what *God* says!

It's important for you to open your ears to the Word of God and turn off everything else so that your undivided attention is upon what He has to say. That is where the victory is. You see, when you close your ears to outside things and keep your ears open to the Word of God, you are closing your ears to fear, doubt, and unbelief.

What we hear is very important, because what we really hear and pay attention to is what we respond to.

LEARNING TO RESPOND QUICKLY

A good illustration of what I'm talking about is an incident that happened shortly after I returned home from my tour of duty in the United States Army during the Vietnam War. I never served in Vietnam, but I was stationed in Taipei, Taiwan, for twenty-two months. One Sunday shortly after I returned from Taiwan, I was in church with a couple of friends who had returned from fighting in Vietnam. There wasn't any carpet in the back of the church, so when someone dropped a Bible or songbook during the service, it hit the tile floor and made a loud booming sound. That particular Sunday, someone dropped a book, and one of the boys dove and hit the ground, because to him it sounded like an incoming round of enemy fire.

When an incoming round hits, all the soldiers around hit the ground! Whoever hears the sound gets down, and it doesn't matter where—he just gets down *somewhere* fast to get out of the way! Even if there is only a ditch full of water, he dives in it! In the Army, we were trained to respond to sounds. And when we heard a high-pitched whistle, we responded immediately by diving somewhere low because that whistle meant an incoming round or a bomb or something else was coming in.

When I was in the signal corps in the Army, we had a signal hut where we were stationed. We would sit in that hut and run communications. The enemy's artillery was always zeroed in on the signal hut, because they wanted to destroy our communication ability. Sitting in that hut, we knew the first enemy shell would probably land just beyond us and the second shell just behind us. So we knew that before they could fire the third one, we had better be gone because the third one was going to land right in the middle of the hut!

Just as we have learned to respond to certain sounds and to other people speaking to us, we must learn to respond to God when He speaks to us.

As a young boy growing up, I learned to quickly respond to my mom when she used a certain tone of voice or said my name a certain way. Whenever my mom would said, "Ken, go do such-and-such," I would say, "Okay, Mom."

A minute later she would say it again, "Ken, go do such-and-such."

In a few minutes, if I still hadn't done what she said, she'd say, "Kenneth *Wayne* . . . ," and before she ever said "Hagin," I was up and moving! I learned to listen to her words, and as long as she just said, "*Ken*, do such-and-such," I could get away with not doing what she said. But when I heard that certain tone of voice, and when she used my full name, I knew I had better respond quickly because the "board of education" wasn't too far from being applied to the "seat of learning."

In the same way we learn to respond to natural things, we must learn to shut out everything else and respond immediately to what God says in His Word! That's what God is looking for. He doesn't want His children to wait but to respond *immediately*.

GOD'S WORD IS FOR THE GOOD TIMES TOO

Let's pick up our reading with Proverbs 4:21: *"Let them* [God's Word] *not depart from thine eyes; keep them in the midst of thine heart."* "Do not let them depart from your eyes" doesn't mean we are supposed to walk around with our Bible stuck to our foreheads. If we did walk around like that, we would run into things, and we wouldn't get anything accomplished. It does mean that when we are facing the circumstances of life—sickness, disease, and so forth—we are to look to the Word of God instead of looking at the circumstances.

If you've been attacked with sickness, you can look at your body and see that an illness is present. But you aren't to respond to that! Instead, look to the Word of God which says, "You are healed and made whole," and respond to what the Word of God says.

Many people go to God and respond to His Word in the bad times, but in the good times they don't respond to God. They don't give God's Word the same attention they did when they were going through a test or trial. Then, when they find themselves in bad times again, they often falter. We need to respond to God's Word in the bad times *and* in the good times! In His Word, God tells us what to do, how to act, and how to *stay* healed just as much as He tells us how to get out of our difficulties and troubles and how to *get* healed.

Again, we need to respond to God's Word no matter what kind of circumstances we may be facing. Unfortunately, many people don't want to respond to God's Word if it means they have to live a certain lifestyle. Knowing they have to live a certain way puts the responsibility on them!

Some Christians even look for someone else to get their healing for them, because they don't want the responsibility of attending to God's Word.

So many times people have come to the RHEMA campus, saying, "I want Brother Hagin to pray for me." I've said to each of them, "Well, I'm Brother Hagin." (And I am *one* of them!)

They say, "Oh, no, you're not the right one."

So I point to my son Craig and say, "Well, that's my son over there. He's Brother Hagin too."

They say, "No, he isn't the right one, either. We want Brother Hagin to pray for us."

Because my dad travels to meetings so much, he's often not in town. So I tell people, "Well, the Brother Hagin you're looking for isn't here." And they reply, "You mean I drove all this way, and he's not even here to pray for me?"

Some people have even cursed at me over it! If a person does that, it tells me two things. Number one, he isn't going to receive healing, anyway, because he isn't looking to God to do it; he is looking to the arm of flesh. He is looking to a man! And, number two, it tells me his heart isn't right.

HEALING IS THE CHILDREN'S BREAD

Proverbs 4:22 tells us that God's Word is life unto those that find it and health to all their flesh. God's words are full of life, health, and healing! The more Word you have, the more victory you have.

Not only does the Bible tell us that God's Word is life, but Matthew 15:26 tells us that healing is the children's bread.

In Matthew 15, Jesus is approached by a woman from Canaan who wants Him to heal her daughter.

> **MATTHEW 15:21-23**
> **21 Then Jesus went thence, and departed into the coasts of Tyre and Sidon.**
> **22 And, behold, a woman of Canaan came out of the same coasts, and cried unto him, saying, Have mercy on me, O Lord, thou Son of David; my daughter is grievously vexed with a devil** [or devil-possessed].
> **23 But he answered her not a word. And his disciples came and besought him, saying, Send her away; for she crieth after us.**

Now it doesn't say so directly, but the Scripture seems to indicate that this woman may have been running after Jesus and His disciples for some time. We know it just wasn't a one-time thing, because verse 23 uses the phrase "she's crying after us," which means she was following after them.

> **MATTHEW 15:24**
> **24 But he answered and said, I am not sent but unto the lost sheep of the house of Israel.**

In verse 24, Jesus says, "... *I am not sent but unto the lost sheep of the house of Israel.*" And Galatians 3:29 tells us that ". . . if we be Christ's, then we are Abraham's seed and heirs according to the promise." And according to Ephesians 1:5, God has adopted us as children by Jesus Christ. Therefore, as Christians, we are adopted sons of Abraham. We've come into the family through adoption, so Jesus was sent to *us* too.

> **MATTHEW 15:25,26**
> **25 Then came she and worshipped him, saying, Lord, help me.**
> **26 But he answered and said, It is not meet to take the children's bread, and to cast it to dogs.**

This woman was smart, and she had perseverance! She was not like some Christians today who wear their feelings on their shoulder and get offended at the least little thing. She had good reason to be offended; Jesus had called her a "dog." He said, "I'm not supposed to give the children's bread to the *dogs*." I don't think any of us would like to be called a dog! But this woman didn't pay any attention to being called a dog. She knew what she wanted, and she knew how to get it. She looked at Jesus and said, "You're telling the truth, Lord. *But* . . ."

> **MATTHEW 15:27,28**
> **27 And she said, Truth, Lord: yet the dogs eat of the crumbs which fall from their masters' table.** [Just a crumb off of the table of God has more blessing than a whole meal at the devil's table!]
> **28 Then Jesus answered and said unto her, O woman, great is thy faith: be it unto thee even as thou wilt. And her daughter was made whole from that very hour.**

Healing is the children's bread! I didn't say it, and no person made it up—*Jesus* said it! He said, "Healing is the children's bread." If you are born again, then you are a child of God. And if you are a child of God, then the children's bread belongs to *you*! What is the children's bread? *Healing*!

Say this out loud, "Healing is the children's bread, and healing belongs to me. Jesus said so." You need to say that until you believe it in your heart and aren't just believing it with your head or mental reasoning. You need to say it long enough for it to register down on the inside of your spirit.

There have been times where I have talked to certain persons for a while and even explained certain spiritual truths to them. They went away meditating on and repeating what I had said. Later, I've heard some of them say, "I got it! I got it! I got it!" You see, they walked away and went over and over what they'd heard from the Word until it finally dawned on them and they understood it.

That is exactly what we need to do with God's Word. We need to get into His Word, and we need to read it and study it so much that we have passages underlined. If you have a Bible you can't write in, throw it away and get one you can write in! In the margin of your Bible beside Matthew 15:26 where it says "the children's bread," you need to write, "That's *my* bread."

I can say that healing is my bread, because Jesus said it was mine. Healing is mine—it belongs to me. And no devil in hell is ever going to keep me sick! I'm healed and I'm whole—all I have to do is eat my bread, so to speak. Healing is *my* bread!

IT'S WHAT'S IN THE HEART THAT COUNTS

The Word won't work for us if it's only in our head. We have to have it down in our heart! I can better explain this principle in terms of what a person has to have in him to play football or any sport. You see, he has to play from the heart, so to speak. His desire to play and win must come from deep within, or he won't ever be any good. Instead, he will go out on the playing field and play halfheartedly or perhaps even get hurt. If he is playing football, for example, an opponent will hit him and knock the fire out of him! To be successful, *he* needs to be looking for someone to hit!

One of my associate pastors at RHEMA Bible Church has a son in the sixth grade who plays a lot of football. He's very quick, but he's not really that big. And yet, despite his size, the kid loves to hit! He can run with the ball well, so the coaches have him running the ball sometimes. But he would rather play defense at middle linebacker than do anything else. When he gets down in position, he is looking for someone to hit! That kind of drive comes from the inside, and it has to be there to make up for his size and keep him on top of the game.

When we get enough of God's Word on the inside of us, we will go out looking for the devil! When he comes against us with sickness and disease, we will stand strong and say, "What do you mean, coming into my territory, Mr. Devil? Get your bags—pack up all of your cancer, tuberculosis, arthritis, and flu, and *get out of here!*"

With God's Word in our heart, we can walk into God's kitchen, open the pantry door, make a sandwich of healing, and begin to eat the bread of healing. Remember, healing is the children's bread! So when you need healing, go slice a big chunk of that healing bread. Smear a little bit of the oil of the Holy Spirit on it! Then *devour* it, because it belongs to you! Healing is yours—right now!

As children of God, we don't have to go to God and beg Him, "Oh, Lord, please heal me. Please help me. Oh, Lord, *please!*" I would have thought my son was crazy if he had come to me as a child and said, "Oh, Daddy, please help me. Please let me have some food to eat," because I had already told him, "Son, everything in this house is yours. It belongs to you." He didn't have to beg me for anything! If my son wanted some bread and milk, he went in the kitchen and got it—because it belonged to him! God has told us in His Word that healing is ours—it belongs to us! We just need to go into God's kitchen, so to speak, and get some of it!

FOUR STEPS TO RECEIVING HEALING

Most people have had to get a prescription filled at a pharmacy at one time or another. There are always instructions on the bottle or tube of medicine to tell how much medicine to take, when to take it, and how to take it. For example, the bottle may read: "Take one tablet every six hours," "Take one pill three times a day," or "Take one pill in the morning and one pill at night with food."

If the person doesn't follow the instructions, he could get in trouble by taking too much or not enough of the medicine or taking the dosages too often or not often enough.

Whenever someone is taking medicine, he must be very conscientious to take it according to the doctor's prescription, because the only way the medicine will be effective is if it is taken properly.

We need to do the same thing with the prescription that God has written for us. It is very simple, and it is found in Proverbs 4:20 and 21. In that passage of Scripture, we find four steps to taking the medicine of God's Word. Number one: *Attend or give attention to God's Word.* Number two: *Incline your ear to God's Word*—listen to it. Number three: *Don't let it depart from before your eyes.* In other words, focus your eyes on what God's Word says about your situation, not on what the circumstances or a negative report says. Believe the report of God's Word which says you are healed and whole. Number four: *Keep God's Word in your heart.*

Regarding step number three—keeping your eyes focused on the Word rather than on the bad report—I don't want anyone to misunderstand me on the issue. I thank God for good doctors. And I believe they help as much as they can. I have nothing against doctors, and I don't have any problem with someone who goes to see one! There is absolutely nothing wrong with Christians going to see a doctor. In fact, going to a doctor does not take away from your faith as long as you are keeping the Word as your focus—keeping it uppermost in your heart and mind. You must simply keep God's report as your focus, and believe what His Word has to say. That's what "do not let it depart from your eyes" means.

Regarding step number four in Proverbs 4:20 and 21, *Keep God's Word in your heart,* the psalmist said, "I have hid Your Word in my heart that I might not sin against You" (Ps. 119:11). We need to hide God's Word in our heart so that when we run into a test or trial, we will take the Word of God and walk on to victory.

ONE DOSE ISN'T ENOUGH

God's Word won't benefit you if you only read it one time a year, anymore than taking a daily prescription one time a year will benefit you! Suppose you had some type of cold symptom a month ago, so you went to a doctor and he gave you some medicine to take. After taking the medicine as the doctor prescribed, you felt fine. Now suppose at this same time next year, you had the same symptoms all over again. If you went back to the doctor and he prescribed the same medicine to you that he did last year, would you take it? Or would you tell him, "Oh, I can't take that medicine. I already had some of that last year."

That may sound silly to you, but that is the same attitude many Christians have when they hear a message on a subject they have heard before. Some Christians can get all excited in the praise-and-worship part of the service. But when the preacher starts to preach, they say, "Oh, I've heard that before," and they start thumbing through their Bible or doodling or writing a "to-do" list! That is the same thing as telling the doctor, "I already took some of that medicine last year, so I don't need any this year."

I have heard my father's sermons and illustrations more times than I can count. And some of the singers and band members who travel with him have heard them numerous times too. But we still keep our ears open every time he speaks. And even though we may have heard the message before, we get something new out of it every time because we are acting on the principles found in Proverbs 4:20 and 21.

Unfortunately, many Christians hear the preacher read a familiar scripture, and they say, "Oh, I've already heard someone preach on that." Then they tune the minister out. You see, even though they are in the meeting, their ears are not open. And that preacher may preach the entire sermon without their getting anything out of it. That minister might say three or four sentences that could change their life forever, but they miss it because they have the attitude, *Oh, I've heard that before.*

The Word of God won't benefit you unless you attend to it continually. These instructions—attend to God's Word, incline your ears to God's Word, let it not depart from your eyes, and keep it in the midst of your heart— imply an ongoing, continual action. It's not something that you do just every so often.

The Bible contains many directives to us that must be done on a continual basis. For example, Ephesians 5:18 tells us to "be being filled" or to be continually filled with the Spirit. And the Bible also says that faith comes by *hearing* not by *having heard* (Rom. 10:17)!

ROMANS 10:17
17 So then faith cometh by HEARING, and hearing by the word of God.

The word "hearing" is present tense! "Having heard" is past tense. There are many Christians trying to get their needs met, their healing, and so forth based on *having heard* God's Word, not based on *hearing* God's Word.

Someone might say, "I've heard all that. He's preaching on the basics, and I'm past the basics."

You can't get past the basics when it comes to faith! Unfortunately, too many Christians think they can! They're looking for new revelation all the time, but they've never lived in the fullness of the revelation they have!

And that's the problem with some preachers too. They think their congregations are expecting them to come up with something new all the time, so they try to hunt up new revelation. But if you're always trying to find a "new revelation," the devil will make sure you get one! And it will have just enough Bible in it to be dangerous.

I've been preaching the Gospel for more than forty years. I was also raised hearing teachings on faith and healing, so I don't know any other way to teach. But I have watched a lot of people get off-track because they were looking for a new revelation. And the devil made sure they found one.

When some Charismatic historians write about my dad, Rev. Kenneth E. Hagin, they always say, in effect, "The thing about Kenneth Hagin is that he's never followed after this or that passing doctrine. He's still preaching the same thing that he preached in 1940 and 1950." My dad stays in the middle of the road, so to speak. He doesn't get in one ditch or the other on any subject. He just preaches the Word of God.

I have heard my father-in-law, Rev. V. E. Tipton, tell RHEMA Bible Training Center students, "Kenneth Hagin is preaching the same thing I heard him preach fifty years ago: 'God wants to bless you. God wants to heal you. If you'll believe God, you can be healed and walk in victory.'"

Let's get rid of the idea that we have to come up with something new. Jesus didn't say, "If you have a new revelation, it will draw all men." Jesus said, "If I be lifted up, I will draw all men unto Me" (John 12:32). Preaching

Jesus and lifting up His Word is what draws people, not any so-called new revelation! It's the Word of God and the Living Word that draw people!

KNOW WHAT GOD'S WORD SAYS

Remember, you don't get faith by *having heard* the Word of God. You get faith to have your needs met and to receive healing by *hearing* the Word of God. Notice it's by hearing the *Word of God.* Some people think faith comes by hearing what all the newscasters have to say. Don't misunderstand me. I'm not trying to tell people what they should and shouldn't watch on television or read in the newspapers. And I'm not saying Christians aren't supposed to keep up with what's going on in the world. Sometimes knowing what is happening helps us know what to pray for. But we can't spend all of our time listening to negative reports and expect to maintain a positive attitude.

It's hard to listen to medical updates and economic reports and maintain a positive attitude. But I can listen to the Word of God which says, "By Jesus' stripes I'm healed" (1 Peter 2:24). I can listen to "God shall supply all my need according to His riches in glory" (Phil. 4:19). And that is how I maintain a positive attitude—by listening to the report of the Lord!

Christians are always talking about wanting to have great faith. No one can have great faith apart from the Word of God. Some Christians won't speak the Word. They *think* they are speaking the Word, but they are only speaking what they heard someone else quote from the Word.

It's not what someone else knows about the Word that will benefit you. It's what you know about the Word yourself that counts.

Also, what some people are "quoting" is not even found in the Word. For example, some people think they are quoting the Bible when they say, "The Lord has given everyone a measure of faith." But the Bible doesn't say God has given us *a* measure of faith—*a* measure could be small or large. No, Romans 12:3 says, "... *God hath dealt to every man the measure of faith.*" You see, God has given us *THE* measure of faith, which implies that we all have been given the same measure. God has not given more faith to one person than He has to another. One person may have *developed* his faith more than another person, but both have received the same measure.

EPHESIANS 2:8
8 For by grace are ye saved through faith; and that not of yourselves: it is the gift of God.

We're saved by faith, and that saving faith isn't of ourselves—it's a gift from God. That's what this verse says! Faith is a gift from God. We all have the same faith—it came from God. Now if we want to *increase* or *develop* our faith, we have to hear the Word and act on it. "Hear" is present tense. So, in other words, we don't increase our faith by *having heard* the Word. We increase our faith by *hearing* it!

People who have great faith simply take God's Word, believe it, and act like it is so. That's what great faith is! God wants all of us to have great faith. Jesus is saying to Christians today what He said to many of the sick in the New Testament: "Go your way, and *as you have believed*, so be it unto you" (Matt. 8:13, Matt. 9:29, Matt. 15:28, Mark 10:52).

JESUS IS STILL THE HEALER!

Since Jesus healed in the Gospels, then He must be in the healing business today! If Jesus isn't still healing people, then He isn't the same Jesus He was in the New Testament. And if that's the case, then Malachi 3:6 and Hebrews 13:8 are lies.

MALACHI 3:6
6 For I am the Lord, I change not. . . .

HEBREWS 13:8
8 Jesus Christ the same yesterday, and to day, and for ever.

God's Word is true, and Jesus heals today just as He did in the New Testament. God's covenant of healing is still ours today! We can have great faith in the Word of God. And as we speak God's Word, our faith will bring us the victory!

MATTHEW 8:14-17
14 And when Jesus was come into Peter's house, he saw his wife's mother laid, and sick of a fever.
15 And he touched her hand, and the fever left her: and she arose, and ministered unto them.
16 When the even [early evening] **was come, they brought unto him many that were possessed with devils: and he cast out the spirits with his word, and healed all that were sick:**
17 That it might be fulfilled which was spoken by Esaias the prophet, saying, Himself took OUR infirmities, and bare OUR sicknesses.

Notice verse 17 doesn't say, "That it might be fulfilled which was spoken by Esaias the prophet, saying, Himself took the infirmities of *one of the disciples' mother-in-law* and bare the sicknesses of *one of the disciples' mother-in-law*." No, Isaiah used the word "our." He said, ". . . *Himself took OUR infirmities, and bare OUR sicknesses.*" "Our" is an inclusive term which includes everyone who is breathing oxygen on the planet earth!

Many people haven't discovered this wonderful truth and received God's gift of healing, but it's still for them! Just as salvation is God's free gift to all people, even to those who haven't received it yet, so healing is God's free gift to all—even to those who don't know it or haven't received it yet. God is no respecter of persons (Acts 10:34), so people cannot say, "Well, So-and-so got healed because of who he is."

You see, Jesus Himself took our infirmities and bare our sicknesses. Because "our" is all-inclusive, changing the pronoun "our" to "my," doesn't change the meaning of this scripture at all. So we can read it, "That it might be fulfilled which was spoken by Esaias the prophet, saying, Himself took *my* infirmities, and bare *my* sicknesses."

THE WORD WORKS!

You can confess that Jesus took your sicknesses and infirmities. You can say it because the Word says it. And the Word also says, "Incline your ear to My words, because they are healing or health to your flesh!"

God always wants to perform His Word in His children's lives. If we will believe His Word, which says, "Jesus took our infirmities and bare our sicknesses," He will watch over it to perform it in our lives (Isa. 55:11).

Jesus willingly took our infirmities, and He willingly bore our sicknesses with those stripes that were put upon His back. Since Jesus took our infirmities and bore our sicknesses, there is no reason for us to still be carrying them around!

The Word has come to heal us and set us free. Psalm 107:20 says, *"He* [God] *sent his word, and healed them, and delivered them from their destructions."* Healing belongs to us!

But, remember, we must know what the Word of God says for ourselves in order to appropriate it in our lives. And, as I've said earlier, no matter how much we know about God's Word, we must never forget the basics. You see, no matter how much we grow spiritually, we will never outgrow the basics of God's Word. And we must continually review what we know on the subject of healing if we want to stay sharp, so to speak, and successfully achieve our objective of walking in divine health.

Always on.

For the latest news and information on products, media, podcasts, study resources, and special offers, visit us online 24 hours a day.

rhema.org

Free Subscription!

Call now to receive a free subscription to *The Word of Faith* magazine from Kenneth Hagin Ministries. Receive encouragement and spiritual refreshment from . . .

- *Faith-building articles from Kenneth W. Hagin, Lynette Hagin, Craig W. Hagin, and others*

- *"Timeless Teaching" from the archives of Kenneth E. Hagin*

- *Feature articles on prayer and healing*

- *Testimonies of salvation, healing, and deliverance*

- *Children's activity page*

- *Updates on Rhema Bible Training College, Rhema Bible Church, and other outreaches of Kenneth Hagin Ministries*

Subscribe today for your free *Word of Faith*!

1-888-28-FAITH (1-888-283-2484)

rhema.org/wof